C000177156

30127 06832552 6

vegan cooking

vegan cooking

OVER 50 INSPIRATIONAL RECIPES THAT ARE FREE FROM ANIMAL PRODUCTS

CONSULTANT EDITOR
NICOLA GRAIMES

LORENZ BOOKS

This edition is published by Lorenz Books

Lorenz Books is an imprint of Anness Publishing Ltd
Hermes House, 88–89 Blackfriars Road, London SE1 8HA
tel. 020 7401 2077; fax 020 7633 9499
www.lorenzbooks.com; info@anness.com

© Anness Publishing Ltd 1999, 2004

UK agent: The Manning Partnership Ltd,
6 The Old Dairy, Melcombe Road, Bath BA2 3LR;
tel. 01225 478444; fax 01225 478440; sales@manning-partnership.co.uk

UK distributor: Grantham Book Services Ltd,
Isaac Newton Way, Alma Park Industrial Estate, Grantham, Lincs NG31 9SD; t
el. 01476 541080; fax 01476 541061; orders@gbs.tbs-ltd.co.uk

North American agent/distributor: National Book Network,
4501 Forbes Boulevard, Suite 200, Lanham, MD 20706;
tel. 301 459 3366; fax 301 429 5746; www.nbnbooks.com

Australian agent/distributor: Pan Macmillan Australia,
Level 18, St Martins Tower, 31 Market St, Sydney, NSW 2000;
tel. 1300 135 113; fax 1300 135 103; customer.service@macmillan.com.au

New Zealand agent/distributor: David Bateman Ltd,
30 Tarndale Grove, Off Bush Road, Albany, Auckland;
tel. (09) 415 7664; fax (09) 415 8892

A CIP catalogue record for this book is available from the British Library.

Publisher: Joanna Lorenz
Editor: Sarah Ainley
Designer: Penny Dawes
Photographers: Michelle Garrett, Dave King, William Lingwood, Thomas Odulate, Sam Stowell
(Pictures on the following pages were supplied by Life File: pp6 top and pp19 bottom)
Recipes: Jacqueline Clarke, Carole Clements, Joanna Farrow, Silvana Franco,
Nicola Graimes, Kathy Mann, Lesley Mackley, Liz Trigg, Jennie Shapter,
Elizabeth Wolfe-Cohen
Dieticians: Clare Brain and Wendy Doyle

Previously published as *The Vegan Cookbook*

1 3 5 7 9 10 8 6 4 2

NOTES

Bracketed terms are intended for American readers.

For all recipes, quantities are given in both metric and imperial measures and, where
appropriate, measures are also given in standard cups and spoons. Follow one set, but
not a mixture, because they are not interchangeable.

Standard spoon and cup measures are level.
1 tsp = 5ml, 1 tbsp = 15ml, 1 cup = 250ml/8fl oz

Australian standard tablespoons are 20ml. Australian readers should use 3 tsp in place
of 1 tbsp for measuring small quantities of gelatine, flour, salt, etc.

CONTENTS

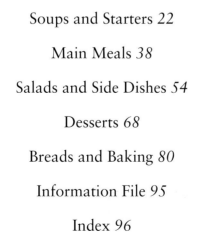

INTRODUCTION

An increasing number of people these days are making the transition towards an animal-free or vegan (pronounced "vee-gan") diet. If you have decided to become vegan, or if you are already vegan, this cookbook aims to provide the information you need to eat an exciting and healthy diet. In addition to using plant-based produce to create interesting and nutritional dishes, there are an increasing number of processed foods available which are suitable for vegans to use.

WHAT IS A VEGAN?

Veganism is defined as a way of living that excludes all forms of exploitation and cruelty to animals for food, clothing or any other purpose. A vegan is often referred to as a pure vegetarian because they have gone one step further than a lacto- or ovo-vegetarian, to exclude dairy products and eggs from their diet.

Most people begin their vegan lifestyle by making dietary changes. Meat, fish, poultry, eggs, animal milks, honey, and the derivatives of all of these, are replaced with plant-based products, such as fruit and vegetables, cereals, pulses, seeds and nuts, and soya products, such as soya milk and processed soya "mock" meats.

Further lifestyle changes are made by excluding other animal products. For example, by replacing leather, silk or woollen products with man-made materials or cotton fabrics.

WHY BECOME A VEGAN?

The most common reason for becoming a vegan is to prevent, or at least to lessen, the exploitation and suffering of animals. Other reasons include health benefits, concern for the environment and spirituality.

ANIMAL SUFFERING

Animals are used for food, clothing, experimentation (vivisection) and entertainment (circuses and zoos). Hundreds of millions of animals are slaughtered for meat every year, including cattle, sheep, pigs, ducks, fish, horses, birds (used as "broilers" for meat), hens and turkeys, geese, goats, rabbits, pheasant, deer, buffalo, whales, ostriches and kangaroos.

Above: The number of pesticides finding their way into dairy milk is on the increase.

HEALTH

The digestive and dental systems of human beings are "designed" for a plant-based diet. A vegan diet is low in fat and rich in fruit and vegetables. Meat, dairy products and eggs, on the other hand, contain no dietary fibre and are the principal sources of saturated fat and cholesterol in the diet.

Allergy to cow's milk is the most common food allergy in childhood, and scientific studies have implicated cow's milk consumption with heart disease and juvenile-onset diabetes. Meat, dairy products and eggs are known transmitters of food poisoning, such as salmonella, camylobacter, listeria and E coli. The artificial foodstuffs fed to farmed animals have an unknown effect on human beings.

Right: Animal milk dairy products are easily replaced with soya milk products.

ETHICS

More people around the world can be fed on a vegan diet than on one based on meat and dairy animal products, and a major shift towards veganism in industrialized countries would bring a radical fall in the price of plant foods.

The typical Western diet gives us more than ten times the amount of grain we need in the form of animal protein alone. At present, 38 per cent of the world's grain is fed to livestock, while millions of people in the Third World die every year from famine.

ECOLOGY

As the world's rainforests are destroyed to provide grazing land for beef cattle, intensive fishing at sea is depleting fish stock, and wildlife habitats are threatened as trees and hedgerows are cut down to maximize farm land. The long-term realities of the animal-based diet are irreparable damage to the planet, and the forced extinction of some of the world's rarest species.

SPIRITUALITY

Orthodox Buddhists and Hindus practise an animal-free diet which is based on the belief that all life forms are sacred, not just human life (as in Christianity). In addition to the ethics of veganism, they teach that a vegan diet is conducive to spiritual peace, and will promote feelings of humility and compassion, the qualities which are most admired in all religions.

VEGAN FOOD PRODUCTS

Shopping for animal-free products is easy once you know what to look for. As well as the more obvious vegan foods, such as fresh fruit and vegetables, there are a growing number of processed products suitable for vegans, from soya-based milks and cheeses to "mock" meats such as "turkey", "chicken" or "beef". Healthfood shops always stock vegan food, and the larger supermarkets are also increasing their share of the market these days.

Food manufacturing and processing is a complex area, however, and it is important to remember that while some foods appear suitable for vegans, the ingredients listed on the packaging may include animal by-products, which are not easily identifiable. Check labels carefully before you buy. You will quickly learn to recognize the more common animal substances, but if in doubt, contact the manufacturer directly. Supermarkets and vegan organizations provide lists of products that are entirely animal-free.

Above: Processed soya sausages have all the flavour of the real thing.

GLOSSARY OF COMMON ANIMAL BY-PRODUCTS

Albumen *or* **albumin** water-soluble proteins found in egg white, milk and blood

Aspic savoury jelly made from meat or fish

Beeswax★ waxy secretion from bees

Bone *or* **bonemeal** animal bones

Carmine *or* **carminic acid** red dye made from insects (cochineal E120)

Casein★ milk protein

Chitin rigid part of insects and crustacea

Cholecalciferol (D3) vitamin derived from lanolin or fish oil

Cod liver oil oil from the liver of fish

Dripping animal fat

Gelatine a thickening agent made by boiling animal skin and bone

Glycerine *or* **glycerol★** a clear liquid made from animal fat

Isinglass a pure form of gelatine, obtained from the air bladder of freshwater fish

Lactic acid (E270)★ acid produced by fermenting milk sugar

Lactose a sugar found in milk

Lanolin fat extracted from sheep's wool

Lecithin (E322)★ fatty substance derived from egg yolk

Propolis "glue" used by bees in hives

Rennet★ extract of calf stomach

Royal jelly food fed to bee larvae to develop the queen bee

Shellac (E904) insect secretion

Sodium 5'-inosinate prepared from fish waste

Stearic acid prepared from stearin

Stearin or stearine★ main constituent of animal fat

Suet★ hard animal fat

Tallow hard animal fat

Whey residue from milk after the removal of casein and most of the fat

key: ★ substance may be non-animal derived, contact manufacturer for details

AVOIDING ANIMAL PRODUCTS

Animal derivatives used in the manufacture and processing of non-animal or dairy food products can be a cause of concern for vegans. The hidden ingredients can be idenitified by scientific analysis, but are rarely listed on the product's packaging because they have been introduced indirectly, during processing. The affected products are wide ranging, and include staples, such as fresh fruit, vitamins and tap water. Vegan groups can recommend products and brands which are known to be animal-free, or you can contact manufacturers directly for details of processing procedures.

ADDITIVES AND E NUMBERS

There are two main categories of food additives: those that prevent food spoiling and those that enhance the flavour, texture or appearance. You may choose to avoid additives for health reasons, or because they are safety-tested on animals before they are allowed onto the market. There are thousands of additives used in processed foods worldwide, and they may or may not be animal-derived. The E prefix used in Europe indicates EU approval. Additives that are usually animal-derived include:

- E120 – cochineal
- E542 – edible bone phosphate
- E631 – sodium 5'-inosinate
- E901 – beeswax
- E904 – shellac
- calcium mesoinositol hexaphosphate
- lactose

Other additives and E numbers may be either animal or non-animal in origin; there are few hard and fast rules in food processing, and the manufacturer is often the only one who will know for sure whether their product is suitable for vegans.

Right: Traces of either shellac or beeswax may be found on fresh fruit.
Far right: Wine, beer, poppadums, dried banana chips and plain chocolate may all contain unlabelled animal derivatives.

PRODUCTS WITH HIDDEN ANIMAL INGREDIENTS

Beer may be fined or cleared using isinglass (a form of gelatine)

Beta-carotene used as an orange colourant and may be held in powdered gelatine

Digestible capsules usually made from gelatine

Chocolate plain chocolate may contain butterfat or may be contaminated with dairy-derived release agents, used to remove the chocolate from moulds

Dried banana chips often glazed with honey

Flavourings may be animal-derived or may be held in an animal-derived carrier, such as lactose

Fresh fruit may be coated with shellac or beeswax

Icing sugar may contain egg white

Poppadums often coated with shellac

Quorn the trade name for mycoprotein, a fermented micro-organism, which contains egg

Sugar production in the UK is free from animal derivatives, but production in other countries varies and may include the use of carbonized animal bone, used as a refining agent, or fish oil, used as an anti-foaming agent

Vegetable bouillon usually contains milk derivatives

Vegetable margarine usually contains milk or animal derivatives

Vitamin D more often D3 (cholecalciferol) rather than the vegan D2 (ergocalciferol). Vitamin D2 may be carried in gelatine powder

Water (tap) some water companies use carbonized animal bone to filter the water

Wine may be fined using blood, bone, chitin, egg albumin, fish oil, gelatine, isinglass, marrow or milk

VEGAN NUTRITION

Veganism is suitable for people of all ages from birth onwards, and there are nutrition guidelines which should form the basis of your diet. Research has shown that the human body can run extremely efficiently when fed exclusively on plant foods. Many healthcare professionals advocate a vegan diet because it can help reduce the risk of the illnesses commonly seen in people who eat a high-fat diet.

A HEALTHY DIET

The vegan diet is typically low in salt and fat and is free of cholesterol. It is rich in fibre (non-starch polysaccharides), carbohydrates and important vitamins.

Research has shown that people who follow a vegan diet have a lower risk of a number of chronic diseases, including heart disease, gallstones, diverticular disease, diabetes, kidney stones, and cancer of the breast and colon. A vegan diet is known to be of value in reducing the inflammation of acute rheumatoid arthritis, correcting intestinal dysbiosis and controlling asthma.

A joint report by the World Cancer Research Fund and the American Institute for Cancer Research strongly recommends a plant-based diet. The report criticises the meat and dairy industries for promoting their products with the message that they are important to a healthy diet, when cancer research proves the opposite.

The following food groups form the basis of a vegan diet. Eating a choice of foods from each of these groups on a daily basis will ensure a complete nutritional balance. A larger part of the diet should comprise cereals, fruits and vegetables, with smaller quantities of pulses, soya products, nuts and seeds, and minimal consumption of processed foods.

CEREALS (GRAINS)
- barley, corn, millet, oats, rice, rye, semolina, wheat, "ancient grains" (amaranth, farro, kamut, quinoa)

FRUITS
- any fruit (fresh, dried, frozen, tinned)

VEGETABLES
- any vegetable (fresh, dried, frozen, tinned)

Above: Favourite cereal foods include bagels, bread, rice cakes, wheat and pasta.

PULSES (LEGUMES)
- beans, peas and lentils (fresh, dried, frozen, sprouted, tinned)

NUTS
- fresh nuts (ground, milled, whole)

SEEDS
- fresh seeds (ground, milled, sprouted, whole)

PROCESSED SOYA
- mock meats, soya burgers, sausages or Textured Vegetable Protein (TVP)

Above: Processed soya products are easily substituted for meat and dairy foods.

VEGAN SOURCES OF NUTRIENTS

PROTEIN

- cereals, nuts, pulses, seeds, soya products

It is commonly believed that plant foods contain poor quality or incomplete protein. While some plants do contain less protein than animal products, all plants contain essential amino acids, the building blocks of protein. Many plant foods, such as soya, millet and quinoa, are excellent sources of protein.

The American Dietetic Association claims that plant sources of protein alone can provide adequate amounts of essential amino acids if a variety of plant foods are consumed and energy needs are met. Research suggests that complementary proteins do not need to be consumed at the same time to be of value, and that the consumption of various sources of amino acids over the course of the day should ensure adequate nitrogen retention and use for a healthy person.

CARBOHYDRATES

- cereals, fresh and dried fruit, pulses, potatoes

FATS

- nuts, seeds (and their oils), vegan margarine, avocados

Saturated fats, containing cholesterol, are found in animal fats and should be avoided on a vegan diet. Cholesterol is necessary for certain bodily functions, but the body produces enough of its own and a dietary source is not required. Most plant foods do not contain saturated fats, with the exception of coconut and palm oil.

Hydrogenated fats, which are found in some processed products, are thought to act in much the same way as saturates and these should be avoided where possible.

Two polyunsaturated fatty acids which are not made by the body are linoleic acid (omega-6 group) and alpha-linolenic acid (omega-3 group), known as essential fatty acids (EFAs).

Above: Protein is widely available in the vegan diet, so long as a range of cereals, nuts, pulses, seeds and soya milks are eaten.

Above: Carbohydrates, such as potatoes, oats and pasta, are easily included in the diet.

Good sources of EFAs include:
Linoleic acid oils made from corn, evening primrose, hempseed, safflower, soya, sunflower
Alpha-linolenic acid oils made from hempseed, linseed, pumpkin, rapeseed (canola), soya, walnut

VITAMINS
VITAMIN A
- (found in vegetables as beta-carotene) carrots, dark green leafy vegetables, mango, margarine, pumpkin, spinach, sweet potato, tomatoes

B GROUP VITAMINS
B1 (thiamine), B2 (riboflavin), Niacin, Biotin, Folic acid, Pantothenic acid, B6 (pyridoxine), B12 *(see section on B12 below)*
- dried fruit, green leafy vegetables, muesli, mushrooms, nuts, oats, potatoes, pulses, wholegrains, yeast extracts and fortified breakfast cereals contain many B vitamins, particularly B2 and B12

Vitamin B12
- fortified products such as some breakfast cereals, soya milks, yeast extracts, TVP

(Claims have been made that certain sea vegetables contain high amounts of B12 but these are usually analogues rather than true or active B12 that can be utilised by the body)

Vitamin B12 is commonly sourced from meat and other animal products. It is made by bacteria living within animals (including humans) and the environment.

Problems that stem from a B12 deficiency usually include an inability to absorb B12 (lack of intrinsic factor). The B12 deficiency occurs in the general population, however, and is not particular to vegans. Only a tiny amount of B12 is required by the body, and stores may last for many years.

Left: Sunflower oil, almonds, avocados and vegan margarine are just some of the foods which will supply the body with the fatty acids it does not produce itself.

Left and far left: A wide selection of raw or lightly cooked fresh vegetables and fruits will ensure an adequate vitamin intake.

It is thought that the body can make its own B12, and recent research has shown that some plants absorb B12. However, further research is required on these subjects before any firm conclusions can be drawn.

In the meantime, the recommended sources of B12 for vegans are regular supplements or fortified foods. The type of B12 *(cyanocobalamin)* used in supplements and fortified foods in the UK, Canada and the USA is better absorbed in old age than the B12 from meat, and people in their senior years are advised to take a supplement, whether or not they are vegan.

VITAMIN C
• berries, citrus fruits, currants, green vegetables, potatoes

VITAMIN D2
• action of sunlight on the skin (5–15 minutes per day), fortified products, such as vegan margarine and soya milk

Research shows that vitamin D is usually poorly supplied in all diets. Action of sunlight on the skin provides a lot of vitamin D. However, if you live in northern latitudes, have dark skin or keep your skin covered when outdoors, you should ensure that you take a supplement or eat fortified foods. This is particularly important during autumn and winter, when there there is less sunlight to make use of. Vitamin D works with calcium to ensure strong bones.

VITAMIN E
• nuts, seeds, vegetable oils, wheatgerm, wholegrains

MINERALS
CALCIUM
• pak choy, broccoli, cereals, dark green leafy vegetables, figs, fortified soya milk and soya milk products, hard tap water, molasses, nuts, parsley, pulses, sea vegetables, seeds, tahini, tofu

Research shows that foods high in animal protein and salt (a typical meat-based diet) increase the loss of calcium from the body. However, calcium derived from curly kale or wholewheat bread is as well as or better absorbed

by the body than calcium from cow's milk. Ensure an adequate intake of calcium (and vitamin D2) for children and teenagers.

IODINE
• iodised salt, sea salt, sea vegetables (hijiki, kelp, nori, wakame), some tinned spaghetti

IRON
• dried fruit, grains, green leafy vegetables, fortified breakfast cereals, molasses, nuts, parsley, pulses, sea vegetables, seeds, the use of cast iron pots and pans

Iron deficiency anaemia is common in all diets. Although iron from plant foods is less well absorbed than iron from animal products, research has shown that iron intake is generally above average in the vegan diet. Consuming food or drink rich in vitamin C during mealtimes enhances iron absorption (vegan diets contain above average amounts of vitamin C).

ZINC
• cereals, pulses, nuts, parsley, wheatgerm

Above: Broccoli, tahini, sea vegetables and seeds all supply calcium to the diet.

Above: Dried apricots, almonds, lentils and spinach make good sources of iron.

Daily Menu Ideas

A vegan diet is more accessible than many people imagine. You can make any dish suitable for a vegan simply by replacing the animal products. It isn't difficult and you don't need to be a dietitian or a qualified chef. Here are some popular menu ideas.

Breakfast

- hot porridge oats or fortified breakfast cereal with soya milk
- wholemeal toast with vegan margarine or peanut butter
- soya sausages, fried mushrooms, grilled tomatoes, scrambled tofu, hash browns
- fresh fruit salad topped with soya yogurt
- baked beans on wholemeal toast

Right and below: Simple breakfast ideas include seasonal fruit with soya yogurt and slices of toast with vegan margarine. Below right: Try a warming bowl of carrot and coriander soup for lunch.

Lunch and Dinner

Starters

- watercress and "mock" ham salad
- sweet peppers stuffed with rice and mushrooms
- red pepper pâté and crackers
- garlic and herb bread
- carrot and coriander soup
- vegetable crudités
- bean and vegetable salad with a vinaigrette dressing

Far left: Garlic and herb bread is easy to make, and is a favourite starter with vegans and non-vegans alike.
Left: A slice of fruit tart served with thick soya cream makes a delightful dessert.

SNACKS

- fresh or dried fruit
- nuts and seeds
- raw vegetables with dips
- crackers, rolls or pitta bread with a filling of your choice
- soya sausage rolls
- vegetable samosas
- spring rolls
- falafels
- spinach and potato pasties
- digestive biscuits
- muffins
- some crisps and confectionery

MAIN COURSES

- spaghetti bolognese topped with vegan Parmesan cheese
- tagliatelle with garlic and tomato sauce
- vegetable and bean casserole
- vegetable biryani and rice
- beany shepherd's pie and steamed vegetables
- veggie burger in a bun with a mixed salad
- mushroom risotto
- spicy tofu stir-fry

DESSERTS

- fresh fruit salad and soya cream
- rice pudding
- sherry trifle
- chocolate gâteau
- cheesecake
- fruit pie
- pancakes with maple syrup
- soya ice cream
- sorbet
- rhubarb crumble
- orange jelly
- chocolate or vanilla fudge

DRINKS

Most mineral water, fruit juice, carbonated drinks, coffee and tea (served with or without soya or other plant-based milk) are suitable for vegans. Coffee substitutes, such as dandelion, barley or chicory, are also popular. Spirits are generally suitable for vegans, but beers and wines may not be, so remember to check with the manufacturer before you buy.

Left and below: For quick vegan snacks, serve sticks of raw carrot and celery with vegetable or soya dips, or TVP sausages.

REPLACING DAIRY PRODUCTS AND EGGS

It is surprisingly easy to replace dairy products and eggs, and there is an ever-growing variety of foods on the market to enable you to do so. You can make quiches using tofu, whisk ice cream using soya milk, and set jellies using agar-agar. You can even eat a full cooked breakfast using soya sausages, scrambled tofu on toast, grilled tomatoes and "rashers" that look and taste exactly like bacon but are in fact made from soya. Very often, even non-vegans do not notice the difference.

SOYA

WHAT IS SOYA?
Soya is a bean related to clover, peas and alfalfa. It contains an excellent balance of amino acids, and is considered the equivalent in protein quality to meat, milk and eggs, which is one reason it has become so popular. Soya has made an enormous impact on the processed food market in the West in recent years and is now used in a variety of products.

WHERE DOES IT COME FROM?
For centuries, the soya bean has been the basis of Asian cuisine, and is thought to have been cultivated in China for over 5,000 years. Many foods have been developed from soya, but the most popular are miso, soya milk, soy sauce, tempeh and tofu. More soya beans are grown in the United States than anywhere else in the world, although other producers include Brazil, Argentina and China. Soya beans and their derivatives are also used for a huge variety of non-food products such as paints, soaps, plastics, adhesives and fabrics.

HEALTH BENEFITS
Soya beans are unique among beans containing compounds called isoflavones. These molecules have structures similar to the oestrogens produced in the body, hence the name plant- or phyto-estrogen. There are many classes of active non-nutrients with estrogenic activity, but interest has focused on the beneficial effects of a group of compounds belonging to the isoflavones. The two primary isoflavones in soya beans are daidzein and genistein. Research suggests soya may offer health benefits relating to heart disease, osteoporosis, menopause symptom relief and, possibly, cancer.

HIGH IN NUTRITION
Soya beans are high in protein, iron, calcium, zinc, B vitamins, vitamin E and fibre. Steamed tofu made with calcium sulphate contains over five times as much calcium as whole pasteurised cow's milk. Soya oil also contains the beneficial polyunsaturated fat. It is free from cholesterol and contains both linoleic and linolenic essential fatty acids.

MILK
Soya milk This is commonly used as a replacement for dairy milk. Various types of soya milk are available, including sweetened, unsweetened, concentrated, ready-to-drink and powdered. Flavoured varieties of soya milk include banana, carob, chocolate and strawberry. Each product has a slightly different taste and most people have their own preferred brand. Soya milk can be used in the same way as cow's milk – in tea, coffee, custard, rice pudding, creamed soup, white sauce or poured over breakfast cereal.
Other milks Rice, oat, pea and nut milks are available from health stores. To make your own nut milk, add a handful of blanched almonds or cashews to 475ml/16fl oz/2 cups cold water and liquidize until smooth and creamy.

CREAMS AND DESSERTS
Soya cream This is usually purchased as a pouring cream, although whipped creams, creamed cheeses and soured creams are also available.

Above: Dairy replacements made from soya include cream, milk, ice cream and yogurt.

Above: Soya cheeses are highly developed to resemble dairy cheeses in all but milk content. Clockwise from top, Double Gloucester, Cheshire and Cheddar flavoured vegan cheeses.

Above: Replacements are now available for use wherever eggs are needed. Clockwise from top left, cider vinegar, soya milk, mashed potato, seasoned tofu and bicarbonate of soda.

Soya dessert A ready-to-use product which is similar in appearance and taste to custard. It is available in vanilla, chocolate, strawberry or carob flavours.
Soya ice cream There are many soya-based ice creams which look and taste exactly like their dairy-based counterparts. They are available in a choice of flavours.
Tofu Made from soya milk, tofu (also known as beancurd) has little flavour of its own but absorbs other flavours well and is highly versatile. Firm tofu is sold in a block, and can be seasoned and cubed for use in stews and stir-fries. A softer set tofu called "silken" tofu is a good substitute for milk or cream in soups, puddings and desserts. For a simple cream dessert, blend silken tofu with sugar or maple syrup, a little vegetable oil and a flavouring such as cocoa powder or vanilla essence.

YOGURT
Soya yogurt Plain, flavoured and "live" soya yogurts are available from healthfood shops and most supermarkets. Soya yogurts are made from soya milk, and are used in the same way as dairy yogurts.

CHEESE
Cheese Hard and soft vegan cheeses are now available, which are made from soya milk. Flavours include Cheddar, Cheshire, Gouda, Stilton or Edam. A Parmesan powdered cheese is also sold for use on pizzas and pastas.
Nutritional yeast flakes These "cheesy" tasting flakes are grown for the healthfood market (unlike brewer's yeast powder, which has a bitter taste, and is a by-product of the brewing industry). Use them to flavour sauces or sprinkle on top of hot savoury dishes.

EGGS
Dairy eggs that are not eaten on their own are used primarily to bind a dish or to lighten it, when air is whipped into the egg before it is mixed with other ingredients. Eggs are widely used in cooking, but there are many ways to replace them.
Binders Mashed potato or a thick stocks can be used to bind veggie burgers, nut roasts and other savoury dishes. Soya milk or soya desserts can be used to bind sweet dishes or cakes.
Raising agents Baking powder, or a mix of cider vinegar and bicarbonate of soda (which is ideal for chocolate cakes) are successful raising agents.
Whole eggs replacers Seasoned firm tofu is commonly used as a straight replacement for whole eggs to make quiches, flans and eggless "scrambled eggs".

THE VEGAN KITCHEN

A varied use of ingredients is the secret of all good cooking. The vegan diet will include fresh vegetable produce and processed products, but you will also need a supply of staples to use as the base for interesting and substantial meals. Keep your kitchen cupboards stocked with basic ingredients so that soups, casseroles, breads and bakes can be made whenever you want them.

KITCHEN CUPBOARD STAPLES

Agar-agar
Baking powder
Bicarbonate of soda
Beans (dried or tinned)
Brown rice syrup
Carob or cocoa powder
Fruit and vegetables (fresh, dried,
    tinned or frozen)
Fruit spread or jam
Herbs and spices
Lentils (dried or tinned)
Nuts
Oats and oatmeal

Peanut butter and tahini
Rice, couscous and bulgur wheat
Seitan
Soy sauce
Soya or other plant-based milk
Tempeh
Tofu (firm and silken)
Vegan margarine
Vegetable oil
Wholemeal flour
Wholemeal breads
Wholemeal pasta
Yeast extract

Below: Useful store cupboard ingredients such as baking powder, wholemeal flour, oats, oatmeal, rice, couscous and cocoa will allow you to make impromptu bakes, breads and pastries.

Above and below: Wholemeal pastas (above) provide the base for any number of quick meals, while soy sauce, flavoured vinegars and spices (below) make easy sauces and dressings to add variety.

GLOSSARY OF TYPICAL VEGAN FOODS

Agar-agar a colourless powder or flake derived from a sea vegetable and used to set jellies or moulds

Arrowroot (kuzu) a fine white powder made from a tropical root and used to make a glaze or sauce

Basmati rice an aromatic rice made in India and Pakistan

Beansprouts beans that have been soaked and left to sprout. Use in salads

Brown rice syrup a sweetener made from brown rice and grain

Bulgur wheat a nutty flavoured cracked wheat used in salads

Carob powder a flour made from the seed of the carob or locust tree and used in place of cocoa

Couscous similar to bulgur wheat but lighter in colour and quicker to cook

Creamed coconut a solid block of coconut extract used in both sweet and savoury dishes

Garbanzo chick-peas

Hummus a dip made from puréed chick-peas

Miso made from fermented soya bean paste; used in soups and stews

Natto fermented, cooked whole soya beans with a cheesy texture

Seitan made from flour gluten and used as a meat substitute

Soya bean a round, creamy coloured bean, similar in protein value to meat, and used to make soya milk, tofu, tempeh, yogurt and other processed soya products

Soya protein isolates the protein removed from defatted soya flakes – at 92% protein, the most highly refined soya protein available

Soya milk a milk substitute made from soya beans

Soy sauce a dark liquid made from fermented soya beans and used to flavour savoury dishes

Tahini a paste made with sesame seeds and used in a similar way to peanut butter

Tamari naturally fermented soy sauce

Tempeh an Indonesian food of fermented soya beans made into chunky tender slices

Tofu a firm white block or cream, made by curdling soya milk with a coagulant

TVP (TSP) stands for textured vegetable protein (textured soya protein). It is made from soya beans and is similar in texture and taste to minced beef or lamb

Wheat gluten *see seitan*

Wholefoods unrefined foods

Yeast extract a salty savoury spread

Yuba the dried, thin skin which forms on the surface of soya milk as it cools

Above: Fresh fruits and vegetables add colour, taste and texture to the vegan diet.

PREGNANCY AND CHILDREN

Many health professionals recognize a vegan diet to be nutritionally adequate for people of all ages, but at key life stages, such as pregnancy and during infancy, childhood and adolescence, the body is working at its hardest, and its nutritional needs should be given special priority. A sensible vegan diet can satisfy the body's needs to promote normal growth at these times. Plan the diet carefully to ensure that any deficiencies occurring in the body are adequately compensated for.

PRE-CONCEPTION

In addition to a varied wholefood vegan diet, with plenty of fruits and vegetables, you should ensure adequate intake of folic acid and B12, preferably through fortified foods or supplements.

PREGNANCY

For all women, vegan and non-vegan alike, the recommended intake of vitamins and minerals is higher during pregnancy. Increase your intake of folic acid, vitamin A (beta-carotene), B1 (thiamine), niacin, riboflavin, B12, D2, calcium, iron and zinc.

During pregnancy the body's store of B12 is not readily available to the foetus, which builds up its supply from

TIPS FOR MORNING SICKNESS

- eat several small meals a day
- avoid fried foods
- stay upright after eating
- eat dry biscuits on waking or during the night
- try herbal teas, such as peppermint or chamomile

the mother's daily intake. If B12 intake is low during pregnancy, the foetus will not have adequate stores of the vitamin, and this may lead to a deficiency in the child at some point after birth.

Human milk is not a rich source of zinc, and breast-feeding infants draw on their own body reserves, laid down during the last three months in the womb. Adequate zinc intake should therefore be ensured.

The increase in calorie requirements during pregnancy is relatively small. There is little, if any, increase in calorie need during the first six months, but an extra 200 calories per day should be consumed during the third trimester. Pregnant teenagers will require more calories as their own bodies are still growing at this age.

Extra water is required for making additional blood for the mother, the baby and for the amniotic fluid. Drink at least four to six 200ml/7fl oz glasses per day of either water, fruit juice, soya milk or vegetable juice. Avoid large amounts of coffee and tea, as caffeine has been associated with various problems during pregnancy.

The basic advice for pregnant women on a vegan diet is to follow the nutritional guidelines established for all vegan adults, ensuring an increased quantity of varied vegan wholefoods. Many women (not just vegans) take a daily multi-vitamin and mineral supplement during pregnancy as extra insurance.

BREAST-FEEDING

The diet to follow when breast-feeding is similar to that recommended for pregnancy, although the intakes of

calories, protein, calcium, magnesium, zinc, copper, selenium and vitamin B12 are slightly higher. Eating an increased quantity of varied vegan wholefoods is an ideal way to give yourself a nutritional boost. In particular, ensure an adequate regular vitamin B12 and D2 intake at this time.

BIRTH TO 6 MONTHS

From birth to 6 months all your baby's nutritional needs will be met by regular feeds of breast or bottled milk.

Breast milk provides a young baby with a natural and nutritionally balanced diet. Gradually your baby will move away from milk as the main source of nutrition, towards her first solid foods.

If you decide to use bottled milk, it is possible to purchase a vegan formula. Ask any vegan organization, healthfood store or pharmacy for details of vegan formulas currently available. Soya-based infant formulas can be used from birth onwards. Standard soya milks used by adults should not be used as a straight replacement for breast or infant formula, as they do not contain the correct amount of nutrients for a baby.

FIRST FOODS

The classic "first food" is mashed banana. Other choices include cooked and blended apples, peaches, carrot or baby rice.

Begin feeds with breast or bottle milk and gradually increase the amount of solid food afterwards. Solids should never be added to a bottle of milk. Do not add salt, sugar or spice to food. Move from solid food at one feed per day to solids at two feeds and so on, following the baby's appetite and pace.

Remember that after four or five months of age, your baby may not receive enough vitamin B12 or D2 from breast milk if your body stores are depleted. Bottled infant formula and some fortified soya milks contain vitamin B12 and D2.

7 MONTHS

In addition to breast or bottled milk, you can introduce blended oats, millet, rice or wholewheat breakfast cereal to the baby's diet, and a variety of vegetables, such as cooked and mashed carrots, sweet potatoes and parsnips.

8-10 MONTHS

Gradually adjust your baby's feeds to fit in with the family's meals. Provide foods which contain soft lumps, such as mashed potato, to get her used to using a spoon. Your baby will be ready for fresh fruits, such as pears, peaches, plums and melons. You can also try finger foods, such as toast or rusks. By now your baby may also be ready to take a drink from a cup. Suitable drinks, other than breast or bottled milk, include cooled boiled water or diluted fruit juices, such as apple or pear.

10-12 MONTHS

Foods should be chopped, finely grated or blended. Your baby will be more inclined to hold a spoon, and may be moving towards eating on her own. A greater variety of vegetables should be offered at this point. Only introduce nut butters on the advice of your healthcare professional if you have a family history of nut allergies.

12+ MONTHS

From 12 months of age your infant can share the same meals as the rest of the family, with additional snacks. Keep in mind the following key points:

Reduce fibre
- cook fruits with their skins on and peel them before serving
- use refined grain products, such as white rice and couscous

Above: Vegan infant formula milks are available from pharmacies and health stores.

Use energy-dense foods
- use fruit juices or concentrated fruit spreads
- use full fat and fortified soya milks or infant formula milk
- make thick porridge and add a little vegetable oil
- use nut butters, tahini and hummus

Use soya and rapeseed oils
- use more soya bean or rapeseed (canola) oil, and less sunflower, safflower or corn oils, to encourage brain and visual development

Boost vitamins and minerals
- use black molasses to increase iron and calcium intakes
- use tofu prepared with calcium sulphate (which contains more calcium than cow's milk)
- ensure access to sunshine and intake of vitamin D2 fortified foods
- ensure adequate vitamin B12 intake
- include vitamin C rich foods in a meal to enhance iron absorption

CHILDREN AND TEENAGERS

Vegetarianism amongst children is common, but many parents still feel veganism is a drastic step for a child or growing teenager. Conflict may arise when different foods have to be purchased and prepared. Older children and teenagers should make every effort to help with any extra shopping and meal preparation.

As a teenager facing hostility, answer any questions your family may have about your new diet calmly and sensibly, and avoid confrontation. Some parents will think it is a phase you are going through and may refuse to take your diet seriously. Others may think it will lead to ill health. You need to prove that your knowledge of nutrition is based on sound scientific fact, and that your meals are interesting and healthy. Once these concerns have been dealt with, the transition towards an animal-free diet should be easier.

You should take time to plan how and when you are going to replace animal-derived products, rather than making a hurried overnight decision. This will ensure you understand basic nutrition and menu ideas, allow your body to get used to new foods, and allow family and friends to warm to your new diet and lifestyle.

The diet recommendations for older children and teenagers are the same as for all vegans. A wide variety of wholefoods should be eaten daily, including fruits, vegetables, plenty of leafy greens, as well as wholegrain products, cereals, nuts, seeds and pulses.

Below: A varied vegan diet can satisfy nutritional demands at all ages.

EATING OUT

Vegan travel guide books list cafés, restaurants, hotels and guesthouses that cater for vegans. The guides are available from tourist information centres and vegan organizations.

VISITING FAMILY AND FRIENDS

If you are visiting relatives and friends it should be easy to organize the catering. Simply explain your requirements, send along some vegan recipes or offer to take along a dish to help out. If you are visiting for any length of time, provide your own staple vegan foods, such as soya milk, vegan margarine and vegan cheese.

RESTAURANTS AND CAFES

The number of places to eat which serve purely vegan food is increasing, but if you can't find a vegan restaurant, you may be able to find one which is strictly vegetarian. Vegetarian restaurants usually provide a good selection of vegan options on their menu. Indian restaurants are also a good choice, as they have a wide range of vegetable-based dishes.

When ordering food in a non-vegan restaurant, check the ingredients of the dish. It has been known for restaurants or cafés to have nothing suitable for vegans to eat, but this is becoming less common. If your local restaurant or café has no idea how to cater for vegans, offer to send them a vegan catering pack. Vegan organizations provide information packs especially for the catering industry.

TIPS ON CHOOSING DISHES

- pizza bases may contain dairy derivatives
- soups may be made with meat, fish or chicken stock
- stock cubes/powder may contain dairy derivatives or animal fat
- vegetables may be cooked in the same oil as meat or fish
- cheese or margarine is typically never vegan (vegetarian cheese is not suitable for vegans)
- few desserts are vegan so choose fresh fruit salads instead
- ghee in Indian dishes may be clarified butter rather than vegetable-based
- unless a restaurant regularly caters for vegans, its staff is unlikely to know whether the wine or beer they serve is vegan

PLANE TRAVEL

Order a vegan meal for your flight when you make the plane reservation, and confirm it when you check in at the boarding desk a couple of hours before take off. Many airlines will provide a vegan meal but you may have to chase them up several times before you receive it.

AROUND THE WORLD

Manufacturing processes differ from country to country, and it is unlikely that you will find food products on holiday which contain exactly the same ingredients as the products you are used to at home. Take with you any products that you cannot live without.

PACKED LUNCHES

Vegan food is not usually available in canteens at school and work, or in motorway service stations. For this reason, a packed lunch is often needed.
- sandwiches, pitta bread, bagels and rolls are tasty, cheap and easy to pack. Fill them with fresh salad vegetables, such as tomatoes, lettuce, spring onions, cucumber and coleslaw, as well as soya cheese, vegetable pâté, "mock" meat slices or hummus
- pack small cartons or bottles of fruit juice, soya milk and mineral water if you are on the move and won't have access to drinks
- vegan pasta pots and cup-a-soups are available from healthfood stores to provide a quick hot snack during the winter months
- small tubs of soya yogurt or jelly are useful to pack for children's lunches
- pack fresh fruits, such as bananas and apples, for easy "desserts"
- sealed packets of dried fruit, nuts, biscuits, crackers and rice cakes provide healthy snacks

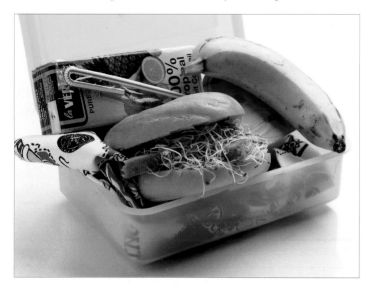

Left: A child's packed school lunch needs to be tasty and interesting. A bagel filled with salad and "mock" meat, a soya yogurt, a juice drink and fresh fruit is a popular and nutritious vegan lunch menu.

ENTERTAINING FAMILY AND FRIENDS

Once you feel confident cooking vegan meals, you will begin entertaining friends and family. Many non-vegans are surprised and impressed by the emphasis vegans place on fresh vegetable produce, flavour and creative cooking. You may even be asked to provide recipes, so be prepared.

ADAPTING DISHES

Any recipe can be adapted for a vegan diet, and there are no limits to the creations that can be produced. Meat is easily replaced with the soya bean substitute for minced meat, TVP, and cow's milk with soya milk. Serve soya cheese and pickles with thick, crusty bread, or mix up your own garlicky mayonnaise with concentrated soya milk, garlic, oil, lemon juice and seasoning. Even trifles can be made by setting fruit juice with agar-agar, topping it with soya-milk custard, and finishing with a whipped soya cream. It is simply a matter of choosing the appropriate non-animal alternatives.

TIPS ON CHOOSING DISHES

When deciding on your dinner party menu, it is a good idea to choose familiar dishes, at least to begin with. If your friends and family have always eaten traditional home-made fare, they will be particularly suspicious of an exotic dish they have never heard of before. However, don't be afraid to be adventurous for more feisty guests.

When catering for your vegan child and her non-vegan friends, avoid introducing what non-vegans may think of as strange new foods – if the food is rejected by the friends, your child will be made to feel different and awkward. Children can be undiplomatic when it comes to food they don't like.

For children who are not used to wholefoods, be sure to use white bread or white rice. Soya sausage rolls made with puff pastry (instead of home-made wholemeal pastry) will be accepted without question. Some companies produce ready-to-eat jellies set with carrageenan (a red algae) instead of gelatine, and these are popular with children, as are strawberry soya ice-cream and chocolate soya milk shakes.

MAKE AN EFFORT

Some non-vegan people may make judgements on your vegan diet and lifestyle before they have experienced it themselves, and it is worth making an effort with the food you provide. There is no need to apologize for the food as well-prepared vegan cuisine is always popular, and even cynical guests will be unable to find anything critical to say about it. Indeed, many people will not be able to tell whether the food they have eaten is vegan or not.

SUGGESTED MENUS

MENU 1

Cream of asparagus soup
Garlic and herb focaccia
Stir-fried tofu and vegetables with
 wild rice
Chocolate cheesecake and soya cream
Cheese and biscuits
Coffee with soya cream

Above: Cheesecakes are a perennial favourite.

MENU 2

Mushroom pâté with ciabatta
Almond paella
Selection of steamed vegetables
Vanilla cream gâteau
Chocolate mints
Coffee with soya cream

Above: Pasta served with a vegan fresh basil pesto makes an ideal supper dish.

SOUPS AND STARTERS

For anyone inspired by unusual ingredients and flavour-combinations, this choice of vegan soups offers endless possibilities. Each recipe has been lovingly created to get the most from its ingredients, and the result is a range of fresh-tasting soups with a wonderful depth of flavour. For unbeatable appetizers, serve Mediterranean-style olives marinated in fresh herbs, spicy Greek dolmades or roasted potato wedges with a hot chilli dip. Or try sizzling stir-fries for a taste of the Orient.

Italian Pea and Basil Soup

Plenty of crusty country bread is a must with this vividly coloured, fresh-tasting soup.

INGREDIENTS

Serves 4

75ml/5 tbsp olive oil
2 large onions, chopped
1 celery stick, chopped
1 carrot, chopped
1 garlic clove, finely chopped
400g/14oz/3½ cups frozen petit pois
900ml/1½ pints/3¾ cups vegetable
   stock
25g/1oz/1 cup fresh basil leaves,
   roughly torn, plus extra to garnish
salt and freshly ground black pepper
vegan Parmesan cheese, to serve
   (optional)

1 Heat the oil in a large saucepan and add the onions, celery and carrot and garlic. Cover the pan and cook over a low heat for 45 minutes or until the vegetables are soft. Stir occasionally to prevent the vegetables sticking to the base of the pan.

NUTRITION NOTES	
Per portion:	
Energy	208kcals/846kJ
Protein	6.4g
Fat	14.8g
Saturated Fat	2.2g
Carbohydrate	12.9g
Fibre	5.9g
Iron	2.1mg
Calcium	64.2mg

2 Add the peas and stock to the pan and bring to the boil. Reduce the heat, add the basil and seasoning, then simmer for 10 minutes.

3 Process the soup in a food processor or blender for a few minutes until the texture is smooth. Transfer to bowls, sprinkle with vegan parmesan, if using, and garnish with basil leaves.

Spiced Red Lentil and Coconut Soup

Hot, spicy and richly flavoured, this substantial soup is almost a meal in itself. If you are really hungry, serve with warmed naan bread.

INGREDIENTS

Serves 4

30ml/2 tbsp sunflower oil
2 red onions, finely chopped
1 bird's eye chilli, seeded and finely sliced
2 garlic cloves, chopped
2.5cm/1in piece fresh lemon grass,
   outer layers removed and inside
   finely sliced
200g/7oz/1 cup red lentils, rinsed
5ml/1 tsp ground coriander
5ml/1 tsp paprika
400ml/14fl oz/1⅔ cups coconut milk
juice of 1 lime
3 spring onions, chopped
20g/¾oz/scant 1 cup fresh coriander,
   finely chopped
salt and freshly ground black pepper

1 Heat the oil in a large, deep frying pan and add the onions, chilli, garlic and lemon grass. Cook for 5 minutes or until the onions have softened, stirring occasionally.

NUTRITION NOTES	
Per portion:	
Energy	244kcals/1031kJ
Protein	12.8g
Fat	6.6g
Saturated Fat	0.9g
Carbohydrate	35.7g
Fibre	2.9g
Iron	4.2mg
Calcium	69.7mg

2 Add the lentils and spices. Pour in the coconut milk and 900ml/1½ pints/3¾ cups water, and stir. Bring to the boil, stir, then reduce the heat and simmer for 40–45 minutes or until the lentils are soft and mushy.

3 Pour in the lime juice and add the spring onions and fresh coriander, reserving a little of each for the garnish. Season, then ladle into bowls. Garnish with the reserved spring onions and coriander.

Japanese-style Noodle Soup

This invigorating soup is flavoured with just a hint of chilli. It is best served as a light lunch or as a first course. According to Japanese etiquette, slurping while eating soup is a sign of appreciation.

INGREDIENTS

Serves 4

45ml/3 tbsp mugi miso (bean paste)
200g/7oz/2 scant cups udon noodles
  or soba noodles
30ml/2 tbsp sake or dry sherry
15ml/1 tbsp rice or wine vinegar
45ml/3 tbsp Japanese soy sauce
115g/4oz asparagus tips or
  mangetouts, thinly sliced
  diagonally
50g/2oz/scant 1 cup shiitake
  mushrooms, stalks removed and
  thinly sliced
1 carrot, sliced into julienne strips
3 spring onions, thinly sliced
  diagonally
5ml/1 tsp dried chilli flakes, to serve
salt and freshly ground black pepper

1 Bring 1 litre/1¾ pints/4 cups water to the boil in a saucepan. Pour 150ml/¼ pint/⅔ cup of the boiling water over the miso and stir until dissolved, then set aside.

NUTRITION NOTES	
Per portion:	
Energy	217kcals/921kJ
Protein	7.2g
Fat	3.4g
Saturated Fat	0.0g
Carbohydrate	39.8g
Fibre	2.5g
Iron	1.3mg
Calcium	28.5mg

2 Meanwhile, bring another large pan of lightly salted water to the boil, add the noodles and cook according to the packet instructions until just tender.

3 Drain the noodles in a colander. Rinse under cold running water, then drain again.

4 Add the sake or sherry, rice or wine vinegar and soy sauce to the pan of boiling water. Boil gently for 3 minutes or until the alcohol has evaporated, then reduce the heat and stir in the miso mixture. Add the asparagus or mangetouts, mushrooms, carrot and spring onions, and simmer for 2 minutes until the vegetables are just tender. Season to taste.

5 Divide the noodles among four warm bowls and pour the soup over the top. Serve immediately, sprinkled with the chilli flakes.

Roasted Root Vegetable Soup

Roasting the vegetables gives this winter soup a wonderful depth of flavour. You can use other vegetables, if you wish, depending on what's in season.

INGREDIENTS

Serves 6
50ml/2fl oz/¼ cup olive oil
1 small butternut squash, peeled, seeded and cubed
2 carrots, cut into thick rounds
1 large parsnip, cubed
1 small swede, cubed
2 leeks, thickly sliced
1 onion, quartered
3 bay leaves
4 fresh thyme sprigs, plus extra to garnish
3 fresh rosemary sprigs
1.2 litres/2 pints/5 cups vegetable stock
salt and freshly ground black pepper
thick soya yogurt, to serve

1 Preheat the oven to 200°C/400°F/Gas 6. Put the olive oil into a large bowl. Add the prepared vegetables and toss until coated in the oil.

2 Place the vegetables in a single layer on two baking sheets. Tuck the bay leaves, thyme and rosemary into the vegetables.

3 Roast for 50 minutes until tender, turning the vegetables occasionally to make sure they brown evenly all over. Remove from the oven, discard the herbs and transfer the vegetables to a large saucepan.

4 Pour the stock into the pan and bring to the boil. Reduce the heat, season to taste, then simmer for 10 minutes. Transfer the soup to a food processor or blender (or use a hand blender) and process for a few minutes until thick and smooth.

5 Return the soup to the pan to heat through. Season and serve with a spoonful of soya yogurt. Garnish each serving with a sprig of thyme.

COOK'S TIP

Dried herbs can be used in place of fresh; use 2.5ml/½ tsp of each type and sprinkle over the vegetables in Step 2.

NUTRITION NOTES

Per portion:

Energy	102kcals/428kJ
Protein	1.6g
Fat	6.6g
Saturated Fat	0.9g
Carbohydrate	9.7g
Fibre	3.2g
Iron	0.9mg
Calcium	57.8mg

Spicy Peanut Soup

A thick and warming vegetable soup, richly flavoured with chilli and peanuts.

INGREDIENTS

Serves 6
30ml/2 tbsp oil
1 large onion, finely chopped
2 garlic cloves, crushed
5ml/1 tsp mild chilli powder
2 red peppers, seeded and
   finely chopped
225g/8oz carrots, finely chopped
225g/8oz potatoes, peeled and cubed
3 celery sticks, sliced
900ml/1½ pints/3¾ cups
   vegetable stock
90ml/6 tbsp crunchy peanut butter
115g/4oz/⅔ cup sweetcorn
salt and freshly ground black pepper
roughly chopped unsalted roasted
   peanuts, to garnish

1 Heat the oil in a large pan and cook the onion and garlic for about 3 minutes. Add the chilli powder and cook for a further 1 minute.

2 Add the peppers, carrots, potatoes and celery to the pan. Stir well, then cook for a further 4 minutes, stirring occasionally.

3 Stir in the stock, peanut butter and sweetcorn until combined.

4 Season well. Bring to the boil, cover and simmer for 20 minutes, or until all the vegetables are tender. Adjust the seasoning before serving, and sprinkle with the chopped roasted peanuts, to garnish.

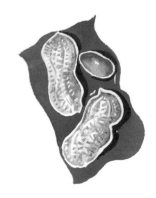

NUTRITION NOTES	
Per portion:	
Energy	209kcals/874kJ
Protein	6.6g
Fat	12.8g
Saturated Fat	2.3g
Carbohydrate	17.8g
Fibre	3.8g
Iron	1.1mg
Calcium	37.1mg

Fresh Tomato and Bean Soup

A rich chunky tomato soup, with beans and coriander. Serve with olive ciabatta.

INGREDIENTS

Serves 4

900g/2lb ripe plum tomatoes
30ml/2 tbsp olive oil
275g/10oz onions, roughly chopped
2 garlic cloves, crushed
900ml/1½ pints/3¾ cups
  vegetable stock
30ml/2 tbsp sun-dried tomato paste
10ml/2 tsp paprika
15ml/1 tbsp cornflour
425g/15oz can cannellini beans, rinsed
  and drained
30ml/2 tbsp chopped fresh coriander
salt and freshly ground black pepper
olive ciabatta, to serve

1 First, peel the tomatoes. Using a sharp knife, make a small cross in each one and place in a bowl. Pour over boiling water to cover and leave to stand for 30–60 seconds.

2 Drain the tomatoes and peel off the skins. Quarter them and then cut each piece in half again.

3 Heat the oil in a large saucepan and cook the onions and garlic for 3 minutes, until soft.

4 Add the tomatoes to the onions, with the stock, sun-dried tomato paste and paprika. Season with a little salt and pepper. Bring to the boil and simmer for 10 minutes.

5 Mix the cornflour to a paste with 30ml/2 tbsp water. Stir the beans into the soup with the cornflour paste. Cook for a further 5 minutes. Adjust the seasoning and stir in the chopped coriander just before serving.

NUTRITION NOTES	
Per portion:	
Energy	263kcals/1111kJ
Protein	9.6g
Fat	10.7g
Saturated Fat	1.6g
Carbohydrate	34.5g
Fibre	9.6g
Iron	4.2mg
Calcium	105mg

Salsa Verde

There are many versions of this classic green salsa. Serve this one with corn tortilla chips or as a topping for bruschetta.

INGREDIENTS

Serves 4
2–4 green chillies
8 spring onions
2 garlic cloves
50g/2 oz salted capers
grated rind and juice of 1 lime
juice of 1 lemon
90ml/6 tbsp olive oil
about 15ml/1 tbsp green Tabasco
    sauce, to taste
1 fresh tarragon sprig
bunch of fresh parsley
freshly ground black pepper

1 Halve the chillies and remove their seeds. Trim the spring onions and halve the garlic, then place in a food processor. Pulse the power briefly until all the ingredients are roughly chopped.

2 Use your fingertips to rub the excess salt off the capers but do not rinse them (see Variation). Add the capers, tarragon and parsley to the food processor and pulse again until they are finely chopped.

3 Transfer the mixture to a small bowl. Stir in the lime rind and juice, lemon juice and olive oil. Stir the mixture lightly so the citrus juice and oil do not emulsify.

4 Add green Tabasco and black pepper to taste. Chill until ready to serve but do not prepare more than 8 hours in advance.

VARIATION

If you can find only capers pickled in vinegar, they can be used for this salsa but must be rinsed well in cold water first.

NUTRITION NOTES

Per portion:

Energy	161kcals/665kJ
Protein	1.0g
Fat	16.7g
Saturated Fat	2.33g
Carbohydrate	1.9g
Fibre	0.9g
Iron	1.0mg
Calcium	29mg

Cannellini Bean Dip

Spread this soft bean dip or pâté on wheaten crackers or toasted muffins Alternatively, it can be served with wedges of tomato and a fresh green salad.

INGREDIENTS

Serves 4
400g/14oz can cannellini beans
grated rind and juice of 1 lemon
30ml/2 tbsp olive oil
1 garlic clove, finely chopped
30ml/2 tbsp chopped fresh parsley
red Tabasco sauce, to taste
cayenne pepper
salt and freshly ground black pepper

1 Drain the cannellini beans in a sieve and rinse them well under cold running water. Transfer to a shallow bowl.

2 Use a potato masher to roughly purée the beans, then stir in the lemon and olive oil.

3 Stir in the garlic and parsley. Add Tabasco sauce and salt and pepper.

4 Spoon the dip into a bowl and dust lightly with cayenne pepper. Chill until ready to serve.

NUTRITION NOTES

Per portion:

Energy	121kcals/505kJ
Protein	5.2g
Fat	6.3g
Saturated Fat	0.77g
Carbohydrate	11.8g
Fibre	3.6g
Iron	1.6mg
Calcium	47mg

VARIATION

Other beans can be used for this dish, if preferred, for example, butter beans or kidney beans.

Olives with Moroccan Marinades

INGREDIENTS

Serves 6

225g/8oz/1⅓ cups green or tan olives
(unpitted) for each marinade

For the Moroccan marinade
45ml/3 tbsp chopped fresh coriander
45ml/3 tbsp chopped fresh flat leaf
  parsley
1 garlic clove, finely chopped
good pinch of cayenne pepper
good pinch of ground cumin
30–45ml/2–3 tbsp olive oil
30–45ml/2–3 tbsp lemon juice

For the spicy herb marinade
60ml/4 tbsp chopped fresh coriander
60ml/4 tbsp chopped fresh flat leaf
  parsley
1 garlic clove, finely chopped
5ml/1 tsp grated fresh root ginger
1 red chilli, seeded and finely sliced
¼ preserved lemon, cut into thin strips
  (optional)

1 Crack the olives, hard enough
to break the flesh but taking care
not to crack the stone. Place in a bowl
of cold water and leave overnight
to remove the excess brine. Drain
thoroughly and place in a bowl.

2 Blend the ingredients for the
Moroccan marinade and pour
over half the olives, adding more
olive oil and lemon juice to cover,
if necessary. Place in a jar.

3 Mix the ingredients for the spicy
herb marinade. Add the remaining
olives and place in a jar. Store both jars
in the fridge for at least 1 week before
use, shaking them occasionally.

NUTRITION NOTES	
Per portion (average of 2 marinades):	
Energy	75kcals/312kJ
Protein	1.2g
Fat	7.3g
Saturated Fat	0.98g
Carbohydrate	1.2g
Fibre	1.5g
Iron	1.8mg
Calcium	58mg

Byesar

The Arab dish byesar is similar
to Middle Eastern hummus,
but uses broad beans instead
of chick-peas. In Morocco, it
is eaten by dipping bread into
ground spices and then
scooping up the purée.

INGREDIENTS

Serves 6

115g/4oz dried broad beans, soaked
2 garlic cloves, peeled
5ml/1 tsp cumin seeds
about 60ml/4 tbsp olive oil
salt
fresh mint sprigs, to garnish
extra cumin, cayenne pepper and fresh
  crusty bread, to serve

1 Put the dried broad beans in a
casserole or pan with the whole
garlic cloves and cumin seeds and add
enough water just to cover. Bring to
the boil, then reduce the heat and
simmer until the beans are tender.
Drain, cool and then slip off the outer
skin of each bean.

2 Purée the beans in a blender or
food processor, adding sufficient
olive oil and water to give a smooth
soft dip. Season to taste with plenty of
salt. Garnish with sprigs of mint and
serve with extra cumin seeds, cayenne
pepper and bread.

NUTRITION NOTES	
Per portion:	
Energy	177kcals/738kJ
Protein	8.0g
Fat	11.8g
Saturated Fat	1.54g
Carbohydrate	10.2g
Fibre	8.0g
Iron	2.7mg
Calcium	44mg

Spiced Dolmades

These dolmades contain sumac, a spice with a sharp lemon flavour. It is available from specialist food shops.

INGREDIENTS

Makes 20
20 vacuum-packed vine leaves
    in brine
90g/3½oz/½ cup long grain rice
45ml/3 tbsp olive oil
1 small onion, finely chopped
50g/2oz/⅔ cup pine nuts
45ml/3 tbsp/¼ cup raisins
30ml/2 tbsp chopped fresh mint
2.5ml/½ tsp ground cinnamon
2.5ml/½ tsp ground allspice
10ml/2 tsp ground sumac
10ml/2 tsp lemon juice
30ml/2 tbsp tomato purée
salt and freshly ground black pepper
fresh mint sprigs, to garnish
garlicky soya yogurt and pitta bread,
    to serve (optional)

1 Rinse the vine leaves well under cold running water, then drain. Bring a saucepan of lightly salted water to the boil. Add the rice, lower the heat, cover and simmer for 10–12 minutes, until almost cooked. Drain.

2 Heat 30ml/2 tbsp of the olive oil in a frying pan, add the onion and cook until soft. Stir in the pine nuts and cook until lightly browned, then add the raisins, mint, cinnamon, allspice and sumac, with salt and pepper to taste. Stir in the rice and mix well. Leave to cool.

3 Line a saucepan with any damaged vine leaves. Trim the stalks from the remaining leaves and lay them flat. Place a little filling on each. Fold the sides over and roll up each leaf neatly. Place the dolmades side by side in the leaf-lined pan, so that they fit tightly.

4 Mix 300ml/½ pint/1¼ cups water with the lemon juice and tomato purée in a bowl. Add the remaining olive oil. Pour over the dolmades and place a heatproof plate on top to keep them in place.

5 Cover the pan and simmer the dolmades for 1 hour until the liquid has been absorbed and the leaves are tender. Transfer to a platter, garnish with fresh mint and serve.

--- VARIATION ---

Fresh vine leaves may be used but must be blanched in boiling water first to make them pliable.

--- NUTRITION NOTES ---

Per dolmade:

Energy	59kcals/248kJ
Protein	0.8g
Fat	3.4g
Saturated Fat	0.3g
Carbohydrate	6.5g
Fibre	0.2g
Iron	0.4mg
Calcium	7.5mg

Spicy Potato Wedges with Chilli Dip

For an easy starter with superb flavour, try these roasted potato wedges. The spiced crust makes them irresistible, especially when served with a chilli dip.

INGREDIENTS

Serves 2
2 baking potatoes, about 225g/8oz each
30ml/2 tbsp olive oil
2 garlic cloves, crushed
5ml/1 tsp ground allspice
5ml/1 tsp ground coriander
15ml/1 tbsp paprika
salt and freshly ground black pepper

For the dip
15ml/1 tbsp olive oil
1 small onion, finely chopped
1 garlic clove, crushed
200g/7oz can chopped tomatoes
1 fresh red chilli, seeded and finely
  chopped
15ml/1 tbsp balsamic vinegar
15ml/1 tbsp chopped fresh coriander,
  plus extra sprigs to garnish

1 Preheat the oven to 200°C/400°F/ Gas 6. Cut the potatoes in half, then into eight wedges.

2 Place the wedges in a saucepan of cold water. Bring to the boil, then lower the heat and simmer gently for 10 minutes or until the potatoes have softened slightly. Drain well and pat dry on kitchen paper.

NUTRITION NOTES	
Per portion:	
Energy	344kcals/1439kJ
Protein	6.1g
Fat	17.1g
Saturated Fat	2.1g
Carbohydrate	44.1g
Fibre	4.0g
Iron	1.5mg
Calcium	31mg

3 Mix the oil, garlic, allspice, coriander and paprika in a roasting tin. Add salt and pepper to taste. Add the potatoes to the pan and shake to coat them thoroughly. Roast for 20 minutes, turning the potato wedges occasionally, or until they are browned, crisp and fully cooked.

4 Meanwhile, make the chilli dip. Heat the oil in a saucepan, add the onion and garlic and cook for 5–10 minutes until soft. Add the tomatoes, with their juice. Stir in the chilli and vinegar. Cook gently for 10 minutes until the mixture has reduced and thickened, then check the seasoning. Stir in the fresh coriander and serve hot, with potato wedges. Garnish with fresh coriander.

COOK'S TIP

These spicy potato wedges are equally delicious served with hummus or a home-made dairy-free mayonnaise.

Spiced Vegetables with Coconut

This spicy and substantial dish could be served as a starter for four, or as a vegan main course for two. Eat it with hunks of bread for mopping up the delicious coconut milk.

Ingredients

Serves 4

1 red chilli
2 large carrots
6 celery sticks
1 bulb fennel
30ml/2 tbsp grapeseed oil
2.5cm/1in piece root ginger, peeled and grated
1 clove garlic, crushed
3 spring onions, sliced
1 x 400ml/14fl oz can thin coconut milk
15ml/1 tbsp fresh coriander, chopped
salt and freshly ground black pepper
fresh coriander sprigs, to garnish

1 Halve, deseed and finely chop the chilli. If necessary, wear rubber gloves to protect your hands.

Nutrition Notes	
Per portion:	
Energy	100kcals/414kJ
Protein	1.5g
Fat	6.2g
Saturated Fat	0.8g
Carbohydrate	10.3g
Fibre	2.6g
Iron	0,8mg
Calcium	78mg

2 Slice the carrots and celery sticks on the diagonal, using a sharp knife or cleaver.

3 Trim the fennel head and slice roughly, using a sharp knife.

4 Heat the wok, then add the oil. When the oil is hot, add the ginger and garlic, chilli, carrots, celery, fennel and spring onions and stir-fry for 2 minutes.

5 Gradually stir in the coconut milk and bring to the boil.

6 Stir in the coriander and salt and pepper, garnish with coriander sprigs and serve.

Pak Choi and Mushroom Stir-fry

Try to buy all the varieties of mushroom for this dish; the wild oyster and shiitake mushrooms have particularly distinctive, delicate flavours.

INGREDIENTS

Serves 4
4 dried black Chinese mushrooms
450g/1lb pak choi
50g/2oz oyster mushrooms
50g/2oz shiitake mushrooms
15ml/1 tbsp vegetable oil
1 clove garlic, crushed
30ml/2 tbsp vegetarian oyster sauce

1 Soak the black Chinese mushrooms in 150 ml/¼ pint/⅔ cup boiling water for 15 minutes to soften.

2 Tear the pak choi into bite-size pieces with your fingers.

3 Halve any large oyster or shiitake mushrooms, using a sharp knife.

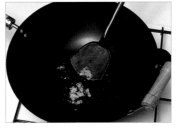

4 Strain the Chinese mushrooms. Heat the wok, then add the oil. When the oil is hot, stir-fry the garlic until softened but not coloured.

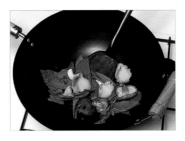

5 Add the pak choi and stir-fry for 1 minute. Mix in all the mushrooms and stir-fry for 1 minute.

6 Add the oyster sauce, toss well to coat the pak choi and mushrooms, and serve immediately.

NUTRITION NOTES	
Per portion:	
Energy	64kcals/270kJ
Protein	3.1g
Fat	3.1g
Saturated Fat	0.35g
Carbohydrate	6.6g
Fibre	0.2g
Iron	2.9mg
Calcium	66mg

MAIN MEALS

Vegans really know how to make fabulous-tasting dishes from the

most basic of ingredients. Cereal grains and pulses, such as rice,

wheat, noodles, beans and pasta, are nutritious and easy to handle,

and they form the backdrop for the wealth of colour and flavour

provided by vegetables, herbs and spices. There are stir-fries, stews,

pastas, pies and pots here: the base ingredients are store cupboard

staples, while fresh produce can be adapted to whatever is available.

Spiced Tofu Stir-fry

Any cooked vegetable could be added to this tasty stir-fry.

INGREDIENTS

Serves 4

10ml/2 tsp ground cumin
15ml/1 tbsp paprika
5ml/1 tsp ground ginger
15ml/1 tbsp caster sugar
275g/10oz tofu
60ml/4 tbsp olive oil
2 garlic cloves, crushed
1 bunch spring onions, sliced
1 red pepper, seeded and sliced
1 yellow pepper, seeded and sliced
225g/8oz/generous 3 cups
   brown-cap mushrooms, halved or
   quartered, if necessary
1 large courgette, sliced
115g/4oz fine green beans, halved
50g/2oz/scant ⅔ cup pine nuts
15ml/1 tbsp lime juice
15ml/1 tbsp maple syrup
good pinch of cayenne pepper
salt and freshly ground black pepper

1 In a bowl, mix together the cumin, paprika, ginger, cayenne and sugar with plenty of seasoning. Cut the tofu into cubes and coat the cubes in the spice mixture.

2 Heat half the oil in a wok or large frying pan. Cook the tofu over a high heat for 3–4 minutes, turning occasionally (take care not to break up the tofu too much). Remove with a slotted spoon and set aside. Wipe out the pan with kitchen paper.

3 Add the remaining oil to the wok or pan and cook the garlic and spring onions for 3 minutes. Add the remaining vegetables and cook over a medium heat for 6 minutes, or until they are beginning to soften and turn golden. Season well.

4 Return the tofu to the wok or pan and add the pine nuts, lime juice and maple syrup. Heat through and serve immediately.

NUTRITION NOTES	
Per portion:	
Energy	309kcals/1286kJ
Protein	10.8g
Fat	23.3g
Saturated Fat	3.3g
Carbohydrate	14.8g
Fibre	3.5g
Iron	3.3mg
Calcium	393mg

Teriyaki Soba Noodles with Tofu and Asparagus

You can, of course, buy ready-made teriyaki sauce but it is easy to prepare at home using ingredients that are now readily available in supermarkets and specialist shops. Japanese soba noodles are made from buckwheat flour, which gives them a unique texture and colour.

INGREDIENTS

Serves 4
350g/12oz soba noodles
30ml/2 tbsp toasted sesame oil
200g/7oz/½ bunch asparagus tips
30ml/2 tbsp groundnut or vegetable oil
225g/8oz tofu
2 spring onions, cut into thin strips
1 carrot, cut into matchsticks
2.5ml/½ tsp chilli flakes
15ml/1 tbsp sesame seeds
salt and freshly ground black pepper

For the teriyaki sauce
60ml/4 tbsp dark soy sauce
60ml/4 tbsp Japanese sake or dry sherry
60ml/4 tbsp mirin
5ml/1 tsp caster sugar

1 Cook the noodles according to the instructions on the packet, then drain and rinse well under cold running water. Set aside.

2 Heat the sesame oil in a griddle pan or in a baking tray placed under the grill until very hot. Turn down the heat to medium, then cook the asparagus for 8–10 minutes, turning frequently, until tender and browned. Set aside.

3 Meanwhile, heat the groundnut or vegetable oil in a wok or large frying pan until very hot. Add the tofu and fry for 8–10 minutes until golden, turning it occasionally to crisp all sides. Carefully remove from the wok or pan and leave to drain on kitchen paper. Cut the tofu into 1cm/½in slices with a sharp knife.

4 To prepare the teriyaki sauce, mix the soy sauce, sake or dry sherry, mirin and sugar together, then heat the mixture in the wok or frying pan.

5 Toss in the noodles and stir to coat them in the sauce. Heat through for 1–2 minutes, then spoon into warmed individual serving bowls with the tofu and asparagus. Scatter the spring onions and carrot on top and sprinkle with the chilli flakes and sesame seeds. Serve immediately.

VARIATION

Use rice or cellophane (mungbean) noodles instead of soba noodles, if you wish.

NUTRITION NOTES

Per portion:

Energy	490kcals/2317kJ
Protein	10.5g
Fat	13.8g
Saturated Fat	1.7g
Carbohydrate	73g
Fibre	1.3g
Iron	2.6mg
Calcium	319mg

Pilaff with Saffron and Pickled Walnuts

Pickled walnuts have a warm, tangy flavour that is lovely in rice and bulgur wheat dishes. This Eastern Mediterranean pilaff is interesting enough to serve on its own, or with a selection of grilled vegetables.

INGREDIENTS

Serves 4

5ml/1 tsp saffron strands
40g/1½oz/⅔ cup pine nuts
45ml/3 tbsp olive oil
1 large onion, chopped
3 garlic cloves, crushed
1.5ml/¼ tsp ground allspice
4cm/1½in piece fresh root
    ginger, grated
225g/8oz/generous 1 cup
    long grain rice
300ml/½ pint/1¼ cups vegetable stock
50g/2oz/½ cup pickled walnuts,
    drained and roughly chopped
40g/1½oz/¼ cup raisins
45ml/3 tbsp roughly chopped fresh
    parsley or coriander, plus extra leaves
    to garnish
salt and freshly ground black pepper
plain soya yogurt, to serve

1 Put the saffron in a bowl with 15ml/1 tbsp boiling water and leave to stand. Heat a large frying pan and dry fry the pine nuts until they turn golden. Set them aside.

2 Heat the oil in the pan and fry the onion, garlic and allspice for 3 minutes. Stir in the ginger and rice and cook for 1 minute more.

3 Add the stock and bring to the boil. Reduce the heat, cover and simmer gently for 15 minutes until the rice is just tender.

4 Stir in the saffron and liquid, the pine nuts, pickled walnuts, raisins and parsley or coriander. Season to taste with salt and pepper. Heat through gently for 2 minutes. Garnish with parsley or coriander leaves and serve with the soya yogurt.

NUTRITION NOTES	
Per portion:	
Energy	481kcals/2015kJ
Protein	8.0g
Fat	25.8g
Saturated Fat	2.8g
Carbohydrate	57.7g
Fibre	1.3g
Iron	1.9mg
Calcium	62mg

VARIATION

Use one small aubergine, chopped and fried in a little olive oil, instead of the pickled walnuts, if you prefer.

Spicy Chick-pea and Aubergine Stew

This is a Lebanese dish, but similar recipes are found all over the Mediterranean.

INGREDIENTS

Serves 6

3 large aubergines, cubed
200g/7oz/1 cup chick-peas, soaked overnight
60ml/4 tbsp olive oil
3 garlic cloves, chopped
2 large onions, chopped
2.5ml/½ tsp ground cumin
2.5ml/½ tsp ground cinnamon
2.5ml/½ tsp ground coriander
3 x 400g/14oz cans chopped tomatoes
salt and freshly ground black pepper
cooked rice, to serve

For the garnish

30ml/2 tbsp olive oil
1 onion, sliced
1 garlic clove, sliced
fresh coriander sprigs

1 Place the aubergines in a colander and sprinkle them with salt. Sit the colander in a bowl and leave for 30 minutes, to allow the bitter juices to escape. Rinse with cold water and pat dry with kitchen paper.

2 Drain the chick-peas and put in a large pan with enough water to cover. Bring to the boil and simmer for 30 minutes, or until tender. Drain.

NUTRITION NOTES	
Per portion:	
Energy	261kcals/1096kJ
Protein	10.2g
Fat	13.3g
Saturated Fat	1.8g
Carbohydrate	26.9g
Fibre	6.9g
Iron	3.0mg
Calcium	93.6mg

3 Heat the oil in a large pan. Add the garlic and onions and cook gently, until soft. Add the spices and cook, stirring, for a few seconds. Add the aubergine and stir to coat with the spices and onion. Cook for 5 minutes. Add the tomatoes and chick-peas and season. Cover and simmer for 20 minutes.

4 To make the garnish, heat the oil in a frying pan and add the sliced onion and garlic. Fry until golden and crisp. Serve the stew with rice, topped with the onion and garlic and garnished with sprigs of fresh coriander.

Mediterranean One-crust Pie

This free-form pie encases a rich tomato, aubergine and kidney bean filling. If your pastry cracks, just patch it up – it adds to the pie's rustic character.

INGREDIENTS

Serves 4

- 500g/1¼lb aubergine, cubed
- 1 red pepper
- 30ml/2 tbsp olive oil
- 1 large onion, finely chopped
- 1 courgette, sliced
- 2 garlic cloves, crushed
- 15ml/1 tbsp fresh oregano or 5ml/ 1 tsp dried, plus extra fresh oregano to garnish
- 200g/7oz/1½ cups canned red kidney beans, drained and rinsed
- 115g/4oz/1 cup pitted black olives, rinsed
- 375g/13oz/⅔ cup passata
- 30ml/2 tbsp semolina
- a little soya milk
- salt and freshly ground black pepper

For the pastry

- 75g/3oz/⅔ cup unbleached plain flour
- 75g/3oz/⅔ cup wholemeal flour
- 75g/3oz/6 tbsp vegan margarine

1 Preheat the oven to 220°C/425°F/ Gas 7. To make the pastry, rub the plain and wholemeal flours and fat together until the mixture resembles fine breadcrumbs. Add enough cold water to form a dough.

NUTRITION NOTES	
Per portion:	
Energy	272kcals/1977kJ
Protein	11.7g
Fat	25.8g
Saturated Fat	6.2g
Carbohydrate	51.5g
Fibre	10.5g
Iron	3.7mg
Calcium	125mg

2 Turn out the dough on to a lightly floured work surface and knead until smooth and elastic. Wrap in clear film and chill for 30 minutes.

3 To make the filling, place the aubergine in a colander and sprinkle with salt, then leave for 30 minutes. Rinse and pat dry with kitchen paper. Meanwhile, place the pepper on a baking tray and roast in the oven for 20 minutes. Put the pepper in a plastic bag and leave until cool enough to handle. Peel and seed the pepper, then dice the flesh. Set aside.

4 Heat the oil in a large heavy-based frying pan. Fry the onion for 5 minutes until softened, stirring occasionally. Add the aubergine and fry for 5 minutes until tender. Add the courgette, garlic and oregano, and cook for a further 5 minutes, stirring frequently. Add the kidney beans and olives, stir, then add the passata and pepper. Cook until heated through, and set aside to cool.

5 Roll out the pastry on a lightly floured board or work surface to form a rough 30cm/12in round. Place on a lightly oiled baking sheet. Sprinkle over the semolina, leaving a 4cm/1½in border, then spoon over the filling.

6 Gather up the edges of the pastry to partly cover the filling – it should be open in the middle. Brush with the soya milk and bake for 30–35 minutes until golden.

Jamaican Black Bean Pot

INGREDIENTS

Serves 4

225g/8oz/1¼ cups dried black beans
1 bay leaf
30ml/2 tbsp vegetable oil
1 large onion, chopped
1 garlic clove, chopped
5ml/1 tsp English mustard powder
15ml/1 tbsp blackstrap molasses
30ml/2 tbsp soft dark brown sugar
5ml/1 tsp dried thyme
2.5ml/½ tsp dried chilli flakes
1 red pepper, seeded and diced
1 yellow pepper, seeded and diced
675g/1½lb/5¼ cups butternut squash
   or pumpkin, seeded and cut into
   1cm/½in dice
salt and freshly ground black pepper
fresh thyme sprigs, to garnish

1 Soak the beans overnight in water, then drain and rinse well. Place in a saucepan, cover with fresh water and add the bay leaf. Bring to the boil, then boil rapidly for 10 minutes. Reduce the heat, cover, and simmer for 30 minutes until tender. Drain, reserving the cooking water. Preheat the oven to 180°C/350°F/Gas 4.

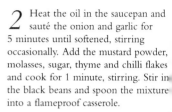

2 Heat the oil in the saucepan and sauté the onion and garlic for 5 minutes until softened, stirring occasionally. Add the mustard powder, molasses, sugar, thyme and chilli flakes and cook for 1 minute, stirring. Stir in the black beans and spoon the mixture into a flameproof casserole.

3 Add water to the reserved cooking liquid to make up 400ml/14fl oz/ 1⅔ cups, then pour into the casserole. Bake for 25 minutes.

4 Add the peppers and squash or pumpkin, season and mix well. Cover, then bake for 45 minutes until the vegetables are tender. Serve garnished with fresh thyme sprigs.

COOK'S TIP

Molasses imparts a rich treacly flavour to the spicy sauce. This dish is delicious served with cornbread or plain boiled rice.

NUTRITION NOTES

Per portion:

Energy	352kcals/1768kJ
Protein	16.1g
Fat	6.8g
Saturated Fat	0.9g
Carbohydrate	60.7g
Fibre	8.9g
Iron	6.1mg
Calcium	150.3mg

Rice and Beans with Avocado Salsa

Mexican-style rice and beans make a delicious supper dish. Spoon on to tortillas and serve with a tangy avocado salsa. Alternatively, serve as a side dish with a spicy stew.

INGREDIENTS

Serves 4

40g/1½oz/¼ cup dried or 75g/3oz/ ½ cup canned kidney beans, rinsed and drained
4 tomatoes, halved and seeded
2 garlic cloves, chopped
1 onion, sliced
45ml/3 tbsp olive oil
225g/8oz/generous 1 cup long grain brown rice, rinsed
600ml/1 pint/2½ cups vegetable stock
2 carrots, diced
75g/3oz/¾ cup green beans
salt and freshly ground black pepper
4 wheat tortillas, to serve

For the avocado salsa

1 avocado
juice of 1 lime
1 small red onion, diced
1 small red chilli, seeded and chopped
15ml/1 tbsp chopped fresh coriander

1 If using dried kidney beans, place in a bowl, cover with cold water and leave to soak overnight, then drain and rinse well. Place in a saucepan with enough water to cover and bring to the boil. Boil rapidly for about 10 minutes, then reduce the heat and simmer for 40 minutes until tender. Drain and set aside.

2 Preheat the grill to high. Place the tomatoes, garlic and onion on a baking tray. Pour over 15ml/1 tbsp of the olive oil and toss to coat. Grill for 10 minutes or until the tomatoes and onions are softened, turning once. Set aside to cool.

3 Heat the remaining oil in a sauce-pan, add the rice and cook for 2 minutes, stirring, until light golden.

4 Purée the cooled tomatoes and onions in a food processor or blender, then add the mixture to the rice and cook for a further 2 minutes, stirring frequently. Pour in the stock, then cover and cook gently, for 20 minutes, stirring occasionally.

5 Reserve 30ml/2 tbsp of the kidney beans for the salsa. Add the rest to the stock mixture with the carrots and green beans and cook for 15 minutes until the vegetables are tender. Season well. Remove the pan from the heat and leave to stand, covered, for 15 minutes.

6 To make the avocado salsa, cut the avocado in half and remove the stone. Peel and dice the flesh, then toss in the lime juice. Add the onion, chilli, coriander and reserved kidney beans, then season with salt.

7 To serve, spoon hot rice and beans on to each of the tortillas. Pass the avocado salsa separately.

NUTRITION NOTES	
Per portion:	
Energy	397kcals/1669kJ
Protein	6.8g
Fat	18.01g
Saturated Fat	3.2g
Carbohydrate	55.6g
Fibre	4.7g
Iron	2.1mg
Calcium	46.2mg

Creamy Leek and Mushroom Tagliatelle

Ingredients

Serves 4
60ml/4 tbsp olive oil
3 leeks, sliced into rounds
2 garlic cloves, chopped
225g/8oz/3 cups brown-cap
  mushrooms, sliced
5ml/1 tsp dried oregano
2.5ml/½ tsp chilli flakes
375g/13oz/3 cups dried tagliatelle
75ml/5 tbsp vegan cream cheese
30ml/2 tbsp chopped fresh parsley,
  to garnish
salt and freshly ground black pepper

1 Heat the oil in a large heavy-based frying pan and sauté the leeks and garlic for 3 minutes until soft. Add the mushrooms, oregano and chilli flakes and cook gently for 5 minutes more until the mushrooms are tender.

2 Meanwhile, cook the tagliatelle in a large pan of salted boiling water for 8-12 minutes until al dente. Drain, reserving 60ml/4 tbsp of the cooking water for the mushroom mixture.

3 Stir the reserved cooking water into the mushroom mixture, then add the cream cheese and season. Heat gently for 1-2 minutes, stirring occasionally.

4 To serve, spoon the sauce over the tagliatelle and sprinkle with chopped fresh parsley.

Nutrition Notes	
Per portion:	
Energy	534kcals/2247kJ
Protein	14.6g
Fat	22.5g
Saturated Fat	7.54g
Carbohydrate	73.0g
Fibre	5.3g
Iron	4.0mg
Calcium	87mg

Dairy-free Pesto with Spirali

Ingredients

Serves 4
300g/11oz new potatoes, cubed
150g/5oz/1 cup fine green beans, cut
  into thirds
225g/8oz broccoli florets
375g/13oz/3 cups dried spirali pasta
2 tomatoes, seeded and diced
25g/1oz/¼ cup pine nuts, toasted
salt and freshly ground black pepper

For the pesto
25g/1oz fresh basil leaves, torn
10g/¼oz fresh mint leaves, torn
2 large garlic cloves, crushed
15ml/1 tbsp Dijon mustard
25g/1oz/¼ cup pine nuts
60ml/4 tbsp extra virgin olive oil
juice of ½ lemon

1 To make the pesto, purée the basil and mint, garlic, mustard, pine nuts, oil and lemon juice in a food processor or blender. Season and set aside.

2 Cook the new potatoes in a large pan of salted boiling water for 5-7 minutes until just tender. Steam the green beans and broccoli for 3 minutes until they are tender.

Nutrition Notes	
Per portion:	
Energy	610kcals/2568kJ
Protein	18.5g
Fat	22.7g
Saturated Fat	2.78g
Carbohydrate	88.4g
Fibre	6.7g
Iron	4.8mg
Calcium	101mg

3 Cook the spirali in a large pan of salted boiling water for 10-12 minutes until al dente. Drain, reserving 150ml/¼ pint/⅔ cup of the cooking water. Return the pasta and reserved water to the pan. Add the precooked potatoes, beans, broccoli, pesto and seasoning, then stir until combined. Heat over a gentle heat for 1-2 minutes, then stir in the tomatoes. Serve sprinkled with toasted pine nuts.

Stuffed Tomatoes and Peppers

Colourful peppers and tomatoes make perfect containers for filling with various vegetable and grain stuffings. This rice and herb version uses typically Greek ingredients.

INGREDIENTS

Serves 4

2 large ripe tomatoes
1 green pepper
1 yellow or orange pepper
60ml/4 tbsp olive oil, plus extra
   for sprinkling
2 onions, chopped
2 garlic cloves, crushed
50g/2oz/½ cup blanched
   almonds, chopped
75g/3oz/scant ½ cup long grain rice,
   boiled and drained
15g/½oz fresh mint, roughly chopped
15g/½oz fresh parsley, roughly chopped
25g/1oz/2 tbsp sultanas
45ml/3 tbsp ground almonds
salt and freshly ground black pepper
chopped mixed fresh herbs, to garnish

1 Preheat the oven to 190°C/ 375°F/Gas 5. Cut the tomatoes in half and scoop out the pulp and seeds using a teaspoon. Leave the tomatoes to drain on kitchen paper with cut sides down. Roughly chop the tomato pulp and seeds.

2 Halve the peppers, leaving the cores intact. Scoop out the seeds. Brush the peppers with 15ml/1 tbsp of the oil and bake on a baking tray for 15 minutes. Place the peppers and tomatoes in a shallow ovenproof dish and season with salt and pepper.

3 Fry the onions in the remaining oil for 5 minutes. Add the garlic and chopped almonds and fry for a further minute.

4 Remove the pan from the heat and stir in the rice, the insides of the chopped tomatoes, mint, parsley and sultanas. Season well with salt and pepper, then spoon the mixture into the tomatoes and peppers.

5 Pour 150ml/¼ pint/⅔ cup boiling water around the tomatoes and peppers and bake, uncovered, for 20 minutes. Scatter with the ground almonds and sprinkle with a little extra olive oil. Return to the oven and bake for a further 20 minutes, or until turning golden. Serve garnished with fresh herbs.

NUTRITION NOTES	
Per portion:	
Energy	370kcals/1545kJ
Protein	7.9g
Fat	25.4g
Saturated Fat	2.9g
Carbohydrate	29.4g
Fibre	4.1g
Iron	1.6mg
Calcium	87.7mg

VARIATION

Small aubergines or large courgettes also make good vegetables for stuffing. Halve and scoop out the centres of the vegetables, then oil the vegetable cases and bake for about 15 minutes. Chop the centres, fry for 2–3 minutes to soften and add to the stuffing mixture. Fill the aubergine or courgette cases with the stuffing and bake as for the peppers and tomatoes.

Caramelized Red Onion and Thyme Tart

This flavoursome tart is perfect for a light summer lunch. Serve with fine green beans tossed in a vinaigrette dressing, and warm new potatoes.

INGREDIENTS

Serves 6
25ml/1½ tbsp olive oil
3 medium red onions, finely sliced
5ml/1 tsp dried thyme
2.5ml/½ tsp brown sugar
130g/3½oz silken tofu
150ml/¼ pint/⅔ cup soya cream
15ml/1 tbsp Dijon mustard
salt and freshly ground black pepper

For the pastry
150g/5oz/1/¼ cups wholemeal
   self-raising flour
65g/2½oz/5 tbsp vegan margarine
25g/1oz/¼ cup walnuts, finely chopped
pinch of salt

1 For the pastry, sift the wholemeal flour and salt into a bowl, adding any bran left in the sieve. Rub in the margarine with your fingers until the mixture resembles fine breadcrumbs. Mix in the walnuts, then add enough cold water to form a dough.

2 Turn out the dough onto a lightly floured work surface and knead until smooth and elastic. Wrap in clear film and chill for 30 minutes.

3 Meanwhile make the onion and thyme filling. Heat the oil in a large heavy-based frying pan. Sweat the onions over a low heat for 20 minutes until very soft and translucent, stirring often. Stir in the thyme, sugar and seasoning and cook for a further 5 minutes until caramelized. Set aside and leave to cool slightly.

4 Blend the silken tofu, soya cream, Dijon mustard and seasoning in a food processor or liquidizer until smooth and creamy.

COOK'S TIP

It is important to cook the onions very gently over a low heat so that they remain soft and succulent. If preferred, the pastry case can be prepared in advance. Bake it blind for 10 minutes, and keep in an airtight container for up to 2 days.

5 Preheat the oven to 200°C/400°F/ Gas 6. Lightly grease a fluted 23cm/9in loose-bottomed quiche tin. Roll out the pastry on a lightly floured work surface, then gently lift it using a rolling pin and line the prepared tin. Press the pastry into the tin with your finger tips and trim the top. Chill for a further 20 minutes.

6 Prick the pastry base with a fork, line with greaseproof paper and baking beans and bake blind for 10 minutes until lightly golden. Remove the paper and beans, then spoon over the onions. Spoon over the tofu mixture and smooth with a knife. Bake for 30 minutes until golden and set.

NUTRITION NOTES

Per portion:

Energy	301kcals/1251kJ
Protein	7.1g
Fat	20.7g
Saturated Fat	3.93g
Carbohydrate	22.8g
Fibre	3.3g
Iron	1.8mg
Calcium	170mg

SALADS AND SIDE DISHES

This range of versatile recipes puts the focus on flavour and simplicity,

with a choice of salads and side dishes that are light enough to serve

with vegan wholefood main meals, or to enjoy on their own for a light

lunch or supper. Simple salad ingredients are given a twist with

special dressings, and cooked vegetables are put together in colourful

composed salads with inspirational results.

Japanese Salad

Hijiki is a mild-tasting seaweed, and combined with radishes, cucumber and beansprouts, it makes a refreshing salad, ideal to serve with a noodle dish.

INGREDIENTS

Serves 4
15g/½oz/½ cup hijiki
250g/9oz/1¼ cups radishes, sliced
1 small cucumber, cut into thin sticks
75g/3oz/½ cup beansprouts

For the dressing
15ml/1 tbsp sunflower oil
15ml/1 tbsp toasted sesame oil
5ml/1 tsp light soy sauce
30ml/2 tbsp rice vinegar or 15ml/ 1 tbsp wine vinegar
15ml/1 tbsp mirin

1 Soak the hijiki in a bowl of cold water for 10–15 minutes until rehydrated. Drain, rinse under cold running water and drain again. The hijiki should almost triple in volume.

3 Meanwhile, make the dressing. Place the sunflower and sesame oils, soy sauce, vinegar and mirin in a bowl or screw-top jar. Stir or shake thoroughly to combine.

2 Place the hijiki in a saucepan of water. Bring to the boil, then reduce the heat and simmer for about 30 minutes or until tender.

4 Arrange the hijiki in a shallow bowl or platter with the radishes, cucumber and beansprouts. Pour over the dressing and toss lightly.

NUTRITION NOTES	
Per portion:	
Energy	68kcals/282kJ
Protein	1.7g
Fat	5.8g
Saturated Fat	0.8g
Carbohydrate	2.4g
Fibre	2.8g
Iron	1.2mg
Calcium	46mg

Moroccan Date, Orange and Carrot Salad

A colourful and unusual salad, made with exotic ingredients.

INGREDIENTS

Serves 4
1 Little Gem lettuce
2 carrots, finely grated
2 oranges
115g/4oz fresh dates, stoned and cut
  into eighths, lengthways
25g/1oz/¼ cup toasted whole almonds,
  chopped
30ml/2 tbsp lemon juice
5ml/1 tsp caster sugar
1.5ml/¼ tsp salt
15ml/1 tbsp orange flower water

1 Separate the lettuce leaves and arrange them in the bottom of a salad bowl or on individual serving plates. Place the grated carrot in a mound on top.

—— NUTRITION NOTES ——

Per portion:

Energy	115kcals/485kJ
Protein	3.0g
Fat	3.8g
Saturated Fat	0.3g
Carbohydrate	18.2g
Fibre	3.3g
Iron	0.6mg
Calcium	76.5mg

2 Peel and segment the oranges and arrange them around the carrot. Pile the dates on top, then sprinkle with the almonds. Mix together the lemon juice, sugar, salt and orange flower water and sprinkle over the salad. Serve chilled.

Warm Vegetable Salad with Peanut Sauce

INGREDIENTS

Serves 4
8 new potatoes
225g/8oz broccoli
200g/7oz/1½ cups fine green beans
2 carrots
1 red pepper, seeded and cut into strips
50g/2oz/½ cup sprouted beans
sprigs of watercress, to garnish

For the peanut sauce
15ml/1 tbsp sunflower oil
1 bird's eye chilli, seeded and sliced
1 garlic clove, crushed
5ml/1 tsp ground coriander
5ml/1 tsp ground cumin
60ml/4 tbsp crunchy peanut butter
75ml/5 tbsp water
15ml/1 tbsp dark soy sauce
1cm/½in piece fresh root ginger,
    finely grated
5ml/1 tsp soft dark brown sugar
15ml/1 tbsp lime juice
60ml/4 tbsp coconut milk

1 First make the peanut sauce. Heat the oil in a saucepan, add the chilli and garlic, and cook for 1 minute or until softened. Add the spices and cook for 1 minute. Stir in the peanut butter and water, then cook for 2 minutes until combined, stirring constantly.

2 Add the soy sauce, ginger, sugar, lime juice and coconut milk, then cook over a low heat until the mixture is smooth and heated through, stirring frequently. Transfer to a bowl.

3 Bring a large saucepan of salted water to the boil, add the potatoes and cook for 10–15 minutes, until tender. Drain, then halve or thickly slice the potatoes, depending on their size.

4 Meanwhile, trim the broccoli stems and cut into small florets. Cut the carrots into thin ribbons using a vegetable peeler. Place the broccoli in a steamer with the green beans and steam for 4–5 minutes, until tender but still crisp. Add the carrots to the steamer 2 minutes before the end of the cooking time.

5 Arrange the cooked vegetables on a serving platter with the red pepper and sprouted beans. Garnish with watercress, and serve with the peanut sauce passed separately.

COOK'S TIP

This recipe will serve four as a side dish, or it will serve two as a main course for lunch or supper.

NUTRITION NOTES

Per portion:

Energy	206kcals/863kJ
Protein	9.5g
Fat	8.9g
Saturated Fat	1.7g
Carbohydrate	23.3g
Fibre	6.4g
Iron	3.8mg
Calcium	89mg

Roasted Plum Tomatoes with Garlic

This light salad is simple to prepare, and tastes absolutely wonderful. Use a shallow earthenware dish that will allow the tomatoes to sear and char in the hot oven.

INGREDIENTS

Serves 4

8 plum tomatoes, halved
12 garlic cloves, unpeeled
60ml/4 tbsp extra virgin olive oil
3 bay leaves
45ml/3 tbsp fresh oregano leaves, to garnish
salt and freshly ground black pepper

1 Preheat the oven to 230°C/450°F/ Gas 8. Select an ovenproof dish that will hold all the tomatoes snugly in a single layer. Place the tomatoes in the dish and push the whole garlic cloves between them.

2 Brush the tomatoes with oil, add the bay leaves and sprinkle with pepper. Bake for 45 minutes until the tomatoes have softened and are sizzling in the pan. They should be charred around the edges. Season with salt and a little more pepper, if needed. Garnish with fresh oregano and serve.

NUTRITION NOTES	
Per portion:	
Energy	147kcals/610kJ
Protein	2.5g
Fat	11.7g
Saturated Fat	1.6g
Carbohydrate	8.4g
Fibre	2.3g
Iron	1.2mg
Calcium	38mg

Mixed Vegetables Monk-style

Chinese monks eat neither meat nor fish, so "Monk-style" dishes are ideal for vegans.

INGREDIENTS

Serves 4
50g/2oz dried tofu sticks
115g/4oz fresh lotus root, or
   50g/2oz dried lotus root
10g/¼oz dried wood ears
8 dried Chinese mushrooms
15ml/1 tbsp vegetable oil
75g/3oz/¾ cup drained, canned straw
   mushrooms
115g/4oz/1 cup baby corn cobs, cut
   in half
30ml/2 tbsp light soy sauce
15ml/1 tbsp dry sherry
10ml/2 tsp caster sugar
150ml/¼ pint/⅔ cup vegetable stock
75g/3oz mangetouts, trimmed and cut
   in half
5ml/1 tsp cornflour
15ml/1 tbsp water
salt

1 Put the tofu sticks in a bowl. Cover with hot water and leave to soak for 1 hour. If using fresh lotus root, peel it and slice it; if using dried lotus root, place it in a bowl of hot water and leave to soak for 1 hour.

2 Prepare the wood ears and dried Chinese mushrooms by soaking them in separate bowls of hot water for 15 minutes. Drain the wood ears, trim off and discard the hard base from each and cut the rest into bite-size pieces. Drain the soaked mushrooms, trim off and discard the stems and chop the caps roughly.

3 Drain the tofu sticks. Cut them into 5cm/2in long pieces, discarding any hard pieces. If using dried lotus root, drain well.

4 Heat the oil in a frying pan or wok. Stir-fry the wood ears, Chinese mushrooms and lotus root for about 30 seconds.

5 Add the pieces of tofu sticks, straw mushrooms, baby corn cobs, soy sauce, sherry, caster sugar and stock. Bring to the boil, then cover the pan or wok, lower the heat and simmer for about 20 minutes.

6 Stir in the mangetouts, with salt to taste and cook, uncovered, for 2 minutes more. Mix the cornflour to a paste with the water. Add the mixture to the pan or wok. Cook, stirring, until the sauce thickens. Serve at once.

── NUTRITION NOTES ──	
Per portion:	
Energy	73kcals/305kJ
Protein	4.6g
Fat	4.2g
Saturated Fat	0.5g
Carbohydrate	4.7g
Fibre	2.0g
Iron	1.2mg
Calcium	87.2mg

Couscous Salad

This is a spicy variation on the classic tabbouleh salad, which is traditionally made with bulgur wheat, not couscous.

INGREDIENTS

Serves 4

45ml/3 tbsp olive oil
5 spring onions, chopped
1 garlic clove, crushed
5ml/1 tsp ground cumin
350ml/12fl oz/1½ cups
   vegetable stock
175g/6oz/1 cup couscous
2 tomatoes, peeled and chopped
60ml/4 tbsp chopped fresh parsley
60ml/4 tbsp chopped fresh mint
1 fresh green chilli, seeded and finely
   chopped
30ml/2 tbsp lemon juice
salt and freshly ground black pepper
toasted pine nuts and grated lemon
   rind, to garnish
crisp lettuce leaves, to serve

1 Heat the oil in a saucepan. Add the spring onions and garlic. Stir in the cumin and cook for 1 minute. Add the stock and bring to the boil.

2 Remove the pan from the heat, stir in the couscous, cover the pan and leave it to stand for 10 minutes, until the couscous has swelled and all the liquid has been absorbed. If using instant couscous, follow the instructions on the packet.

3 Tip the couscous into a bowl. Stir in the tomatoes, parsley, mint, chilli and lemon juice, with salt and pepper to taste. If possible, leave to stand for up to an hour to allow the flavours to develop fully.

4 To serve, line a bowl with crisp lettuce leaves and spoon the couscous salad into the centre. Scatter over the toasted pine nuts and grated lemon rind, to garnish.

NUTRITION NOTES	
Per portion:	
Energy	185kcals/772kJ
Protein	3.2g
Fat	8.9g
Saturated Fat	1.2g
Carbohydrate	24.4g
Fibre	0.6g
Iron	3.1mg
Calcium	26mg

Broccoli with Soy Sauce

A wonderfully simple dish that you will want to make again and again. The broccoli cooks in minutes, so don't start cooking until you are almost ready to eat.

INGREDIENTS

Serves 4
450g/1lb broccoli
15ml/1 tbsp vegetable oil
2 garlic cloves, crushed
30ml/2 tbsp light soy sauce
salt
fried garlic slices, to garnish

1 Trim the thick stems of the broccoli and cut the head into large florets.

2 Bring a large saucepan of salted water to the boil. Add the broccoli and cook for 3–4 minutes until crisp and tender.

3 Drain the broccoli, arrange in a serving dish and keep warm.

4 Heat the oil in a small saucepan. Fry the garlic for 2 minutes to release the flavour, then remove it with a slotted spoon. Pour the hot oil carefully over the broccoli, taking care as it will splatter. Drizzle the soy sauce over the broccoli, scatter over the fried garlic and serve.

NUTRITION NOTES	
Per portion:	
Energy	61kcals/394kJ
Protein	4.9g
Fat	3.8g
Saturated Fat	0.5g
Carbohydrate	2.0g
Fibre	2.9g
Iron	1.9mg
Calcium	63mg

Glazed Sweet Potatoes with Ginger and Allspice

Fried sweet potatoes acquire a candied coating when cooked with ginger, syrup and allspice. Cayenne pepper cuts through the sweetness.

INGREDIENTS

Serves 4
900g/2lb sweet potatoes
25g/1oz/2 tbsp vegan margarine
45ml/3 tbsp olive oil
2 garlic cloves, crushed
2 pieces of stem ginger,
    roughly chopped
10ml/2 tsp ground allspice
15ml/1 tbsp syrup from stem ginger jar
10ml/2 tsp chopped fresh thyme, plus
    extra sprigs to garnish
salt and cayenne pepper

1 Peel the sweet potatoes and cut into 1cm/½in cubes. Melt the margarine with the oil in a frying pan. Add the sweet potato cubes and fry for 10 minutes, until just soft.

NUTRITION NOTES	
Per portion:	
Energy	327kcals/1379kJ
Protein	2.7g
Fat	14.0g
Saturated Fat	2.9g
Carbohydrate	50.9g
Fibre	5.4g
Iron	1.6mg
Calcium	54.7mg

2 Stir in the garlic, ginger and allspice. Cook, stirring, for 5 minutes more. Stir in the ginger syrup, salt, a generous pinch of cayenne pepper and the fresh thyme. Stir for 1-2 minutes more, then serve scattered with thyme sprigs.

Roasted Root Vegetables with Whole Spice Seeds

These spicy root vegetables are delicious served as the main part of a meal with rice or couscous, or as a side dish.

INGREDIENTS

Serves 4
3 parsnips, peeled
3 potatoes, peeled
3 carrots, peeled
3 sweet potatoes, peeled
60ml/4 tbsp olive oil
8 shallots, peeled
2 garlic cloves, sliced
10ml/2 tsp white mustard seeds
10ml/2 tsp coriander seeds, lightly
    crushed
5ml/1 tsp cumin seeds
2 bay leaves
salt and ground black pepper

1 Preheat the oven to 190°C/ 375°F/Gas 5. Bring a saucepan of lightly salted water to the boil. Cut the parsnips, potatoes, carrots and sweet potatoes into chunks. Add them to the pan and bring the water back to the boil. Boil for 2 minutes, then drain the vegetables thoroughly.

2 Pour the olive oil into a large heavy roasting tin and place over a moderate heat. Add the vegetables, shallots and garlic. Fry, tossing the vegetables over the heat until they are pale golden at the edges.

VARIATION
Vary the selection of vegetables according to what is available. Try using swede or pumpkin instead of, or as well as, the vegetables suggested here.

3 Add the mustard seeds, coriander seeds, cumin seeds and bay leaves. Cook for 1 minute, then season to taste with salt and pepper. Transfer the roasting tin to the oven and roast for 45 minutes, turning occasionally, until the vegetables are crisp and golden and cooked through.

NUTRITION NOTES	
Per portion:	
Energy	234kcals/979kJ
Protein	3.4g
Fat	12.1g
Saturated Fat	1.8g
Carbohydrate	29.5g
Fibre	4.6g
Iron	0.9mg
Calcium	45mg

Rice with Dill and Broad Beans

This is a favourite rice dish in Iran, where it is called *baghali polo*. The combination of broad beans, dill and warm spices works very well, and the saffron rice adds a splash of bright colour.

INGREDIENTS

Serves 4

275g/10oz/1½ cups basmati rice, soaked
750ml/1¼ pints/3 cups water
40g/1½oz/3 tbsp melted vegan margarine
175g/6oz/1½ cups frozen baby broad beans, thawed and peeled
90ml/6 tbsp finely chopped fresh dill, plus 1 fresh dill sprig, to garnish
5ml/1 tsp ground cinnamon
5ml/1 tsp ground cumin
2–3 saffron strands, soaked in 15ml/1 tbsp boiling water
salt

1 Drain the rice, put it into a pan and pour in the measured water. Add a little salt. Bring to the boil, then lower the heat and simmer very gently for 10 minutes. Drain, rinse in warm water and drain once again.

2 Melt the margarine in a non-stick saucepan. Pour two-thirds of the melted margarine into a small jug and set aside. Spoon enough rice into the pan to cover the bottom. Add a quarter of the beans and a little dill. Spread over another layer of rice, then a layer of beans and dill. Repeat the layers until all the beans and dill have been used up, ending with a layer of rice. Cook over a gentle heat for 8 minutes until nearly tender.

3 Pour the reserved melted margarine over the rice. Sprinkle with the ground cinnamon and cumin. Cover the pan with a clean dish towel and a tight-fitting lid, lifting the corners of the cloth back over the lid. Cook over a low heat for 25–30 minutes.

4 Spoon about 45ml/3 tbsp of the cooked rice into the bowl of saffron water; mix well. Mound the remaining rice mixture on a large serving plate and spoon the saffron rice on one side to decorate. Serve at once, decorated with a sprig of fresh dill.

NUTRITION NOTES	
Per portion:	
Energy	346kcals/1444kJ
Protein	76g
Fat	8.9g
Saturated Fat	2.5g
Carbohydrate	58g
Fibre	2.6g
Iron	1.3mg
Calcium	23.5mg

Mushroom Pilau

This dish is simplicity itself. Serve with an Indian vegetable or lentil dish and warmed naan bread.

INGREDIENTS

Serves 4
45ml/3 tbsp vegetable oil
2 shallots, finely chopped
1 garlic clove, crushed
3 green cardamom pods
175g/6oz/2¼ cups button mushrooms, sliced
225g/8oz/generous 1 cup basmati rice, soaked
5ml/1 tsp grated fresh root ginger
good pinch of garam masala
450ml/¾ pint/scant 2 cups water
15ml/1 tbsp chopped fresh coriander
salt

1 Heat the oil in a flameproof casserole and fry the shallots, garlic and cardamom pods over a medium heat for 3–4 minutes until the shallots have softened and are beginning to brown.

2 Add the mushrooms and fry for 2–3 minutes more. Add the rice, ginger and garam masala. Stir-fry over a low heat for 2 minutes, then stir in the water and salt. Bring to the boil, cover and simmer for 10 minutes.

3 Remove the casserole from the heat. Leave to stand, covered, for 5 minutes. Add the chopped coriander and fork it through the rice. Spoon into a serving bowl and serve at once.

NUTRITION NOTES	
Per portion:	
Energy	285kcals/1601kJ
Protein	5.1g
Fat	8.7g
Saturated Fat	0.9g
Carbohydrate	45.7g
Fibre	0.5g
Iron	1.0mg
Calcium	15.7mg

DESSERTS

This collection is proof that you don't need to be a dairy food eater to
enjoy elaborate desserts. Simple poached fruit on its own is all that
some menus need as a sweetener, but for occasions where a touch of
luxury is needed, choose from one of the sensational vegan desserts
included here. Sorbets, ice creams, cheesecakes, crumbles and fruit tarts
are all easily achievable using soya milk products in place of dairy
milk, cream and eggs.

Strawberry and Vanilla Tofu Ice

This pretty pink dairy-free ice cream has a remarkably creamy taste. Serve with slices of fresh strawberry, or in a cone, drizzled with strawberry syrup.

INGREDIENTS

Serves 8
450ml/¾ pint/scant 2 cups soya milk
50g/2oz/¼ cup caster sugar
20ml/4 tsp cornflour
5ml/1 tsp vanilla essence
500g/1¼lb silken tofu
15ml/1 tbsp sunflower oil
30ml/2 tbsp maple syrup
250g/9oz/2 cups strawberries, hulled
  and halved

1 Reserve 60ml/4 tbsp soya milk, then pour the remainder into a large saucepan, and bring to the boil. Blend the sugar and cornflour with the reserved milk in a bowl. Add the sugar mixture and vanilla essence to the warm milk. Simmer, stirring, for 2 minutes until thickened.

2 Pour the mixture into a bowl, cover with a sheet of greaseproof paper to prevent a skin forming, then leave to cool.

3 Blend the silken tofu, sunflower oil, maple syrup and strawberries, reserving a few of the best ones to decorate, in a food processor or blender until smooth and creamy.

4 Add the strawberry mixture to the cooled custard and mix to combine. Pour the mixture into a freezer-proof container and freeze for 2 hours.

5 Whisk the half-frozen mixture until smooth, then return to the freezer for a further hour. Whisk again and freeze until solid. Remove the ice cream from the freezer 20 minutes before serving to allow it to soften.

NUTRITION NOTES	
Per portion:	
Energy	135kcals/565kJ
Protein	7.0g
Fat	5.4g
Saturated Fat	0.73g
Carbohydrate	15.3g
Fibre	0.3g
Iron	1.8mg
Calcium	365mg

VARIATION
Substitute the strawberries with raspberries, mango or peaches, if preferred.

Chocolate Sorbet with Red Fruits

The chill that thrills, that's chocolate sorbet. For a really fine texture, it helps to have an ice cream maker, which churns the mixture as it freezes, but you can make it by hand quite easily.

INGREDIENTS

Serves 6

475ml/16fl oz/2 cups water
45ml/3 tbsp maple syrup
115g/4oz/generous ½ cup caster sugar
75g/3oz/¾ cup cocoa powder
50g/2oz plain dark chocolate, broken
  into squares
400g/14oz soft red fruits, such as
  raspberries, redcurrants or
  strawberries, to serve

1 Place the water, maple syrup, sugar and cocoa in a saucepan. Heat gently, stirring occasionally, until the sugar has completely dissolved.

2 Remove from the heat, add the chocolate and stir until melted. Leave until cool.

3 Tip into an ice cream maker and churn until frozen. Alternatively, pour into a freezer-proof container and freeze until slushy, then whisk until smooth and freeze again for a further hour. Whisk again and freeze until solid.

4 Remove from the freezer 10–15 minutes before serving, so that the sorbet softens slightly. Serve in scoops, with the soft fruits.

COOK'S TIP

This sorbet looks attractive if served in small oval scoops shaped with two spoons. Simply scoop out the sorbet with one tablespoon, then use another to smooth it off and transfer to a plate.

NUTRITION NOTES	
Per portion:	
Energy	199kcals/837kJ
Protein	3.6g
Fat	5.2g
Saturated Fat	2.94g
Carbohydrate	36.6g
Fibre	3.7g
Iron	2.3mg
Calcium	57mg

Pears with Ginger and Star Anise

Star anise and ginger give a refreshing twist to this traditional recipe for poached pears. Serve slightly chilled, with soya yogurt.

INGREDIENTS

serves 4

75g/3oz/6 tbsp caster sugar
300ml/½ pint/1¼ cups white
   dessert wine
thinly pared rind and juice of
   1 lemon
7.5cm/3in piece of fresh root
   ginger, bruised
5 star anise
10 cloves
600ml/1 pint/2½ cups water
6 slightly unripe pears
25g/1oz/3 tbsp drained, stem
   ginger in syrup, sliced
thick soya yogurt, to serve

1 Place the caster sugar, dessert wine, lemon rind and juice, fresh root ginger, star anise, cloves and water into a saucepan just large enough to hold the pears snugly in an upright position. Bring to the boil.

2 Meanwhile, peel the pears, leaving the stems intact. Add them to the wine mixture, making sure that they are totally immersed in the liquid.

3 Return the wine mixture to the boil, lower the heat, cover and simmer for 15–20 minutes, or until the pears are tender. Lift out the pears with a slotted spoon and place them in a heatproof dish. Boil the wine syrup rapidly until it is reduced by about half, then pour over the pears. Allow them to cool, then chill.

4 Cut the pears into thick slices and arrange these on four serving plates. Remove the ginger and whole spices from the wine sauce, stir in the preserved ginger and spoon the sauce over the pears. Serve with soya yogurt.

NUTRITION NOTES	
Per portion:	
Energy	190kcals/807kJ
Protein	0.9g
Fat	0.3g
Saturated Fat	0.0g
Carbohydrate	45.2g
Fibre	5.3g
Iron	0.7mg
Calcium	32mg

Tapioca and Taro Pudding

This pudding is light and surprisingly refreshing, and is popular with children and adults alike. Serve it warm or chilled.

INGREDIENTS

Serves 4–6
115g/4oz/⅔ cup tapioca
1.5litres/2½ pints/6¼ cups water
225g/8oz taro
150g/5oz/⅔ cup rock sugar
300ml/½ pint/1¼ cups coconut milk

1 Rinse and drain the tapioca, then place in a bowl with fresh water to cover. Leave to soak for 30 minutes.

2 Drain the tapioca and put it in a saucepan with 900ml/1½ pints/3¾ cups water. Bring to the boil, then lower the heat and simmer for about 6 minutes, or until the tapioca is transparent. Drain, refresh under cold water, and drain again.

3 Peel the taro and cut it into diamond-shaped slices, about 1cm/½in thick. Pour the remaining water into a saucepan and bring it to the boil. Add the taro and cook for 10–15 minutes or until it is just tender.

4 Using a slotted spoon, lift out half of the taro slices and set them aside. Continue to cook the remaining taro until it is very soft, then tip the taro and cooking liquid into a food processor or blender and process until completely smooth.

5 Return the taro "soup" to the clean pan; stir in the sugar and simmer, stirring occasionally, until the sugar has dissolved.

6 Stir in the tapioca, reserved taro and coconut milk. Cook for a few minutes. Serve immediately in heated bowls. Alternatively, cool and chill before serving.

--- COOK'S TIP ---

Taro is a starchy tuber that tastes rather like a floury potato. If it is difficult to obtain, use sweet potato instead.

--- NUTRITION NOTES ---

Per portion (if serving 4):

Energy	457kcals/1952kJ
Protein	0.6g
Fat	0.3g
Saturated Fat	0.2g
Carbohydrate	122g
Fibre	0.9g
Iron	0.3g
Calcium	49.5mg

Tropical Mango and Pecan Cheesecake

This cheesecake is so rich and creamy, it is hard to believe it's completely dairy-free. Sometimes it's nice to be naughty!

INGREDIENTS

Serves 8
65g/2½oz/5 tbsp vegan margarine
175g/6oz/½ cup vegan oat biscuits, crushed
40g/1½oz/¼ cup ground almonds
1 large mango, diced
juice of 1 lemon
200g/7oz/scant 1 cup natural soya yogurt
15ml/1 tbsp cornflour
45ml/3 tbsp maple syrup
2 x 225g/8 oz tub vegan cream cheese

For the topping
50g/2oz/½ cup shelled pecan nuts
30ml/2 tbsp maple syrup
1 mango, diced

1 Preheat the oven to 180°C/350°F/ Gas 4. To make the cheesecake base, melt the margarine in a saucepan, then stir in the crushed biscuits and ground almonds. Press the biscuit mixture into the base of a deep, lightly greased 23cm/9in loose-bottomed cake tin. Cook in the preheated oven for 10 minutes.

2 Meanwhile, blend the mango, lemon juice, yogurt, cornflour, maple syrup and vegan cream cheese in a food processor until smooth. Pour the mixture over the biscuit base and smooth with the back of a spoon. Bake for 25–30 minutes, until lightly golden and set. Allow to cool in the tin, then transfer to a wire rack and refrigerate until ready to serve.

3 To make the topping, toast the pecan nuts in a dry frying pan for 2-3 minutes until browned. Heat the maple syrup in a separate pan, then add to the pecan nuts in the frying pan. Stir well to coat. Remove from the heat and brush the top of the cheesecake with the maple syrup.

4 Arrange the pecan nuts around the edge of the cheesecake, reserving a few to decorate the centre. Arrange the mango inside the outer circle of nuts. Pour over any remaining maple syrup.

NUTRITION NOTES	
Per portion:	
Energy	589kcals/2439kJ
Protein	6.6g
Fat	47.7g
Saturated Fat	20.34g
Carbohydrate	35.4g
Fibre	2.9g
Iron	1.7mg
Calcium	108mg

— COOK'S TIP —

Vegan cream cheese is now widely available in health food shops. It is usually a mixture of soya and vegetable oils.

Orange Blossom Jelly

A fresh orange jelly makes a delightful dessert. The natural fruit flavour combined with the smooth jelly has a cleansing quality that is especially welcome after a rich main course. Serve with thin crisp biscuits.

INGREDIENTS

Serves 4–6

65g/2½oz/5 tbsp caster sugar
150ml/¼ pint/⅔ cup water
18ml/3 heaped tsp vegetable gelling
   powder
600ml/1 pint/2½ cups freshly squeezed
   orange juice
30ml/2 tbsp orange flower water

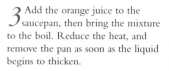

1 Place the caster sugar and water in a small saucepan and gently heat to dissolve the sugar. Leave to cool.

2 Sprinkle over the vegetable gelling powder and mix well until it is incorporated.

3 Add the orange juice to the saucepan, then bring the mixture to the boil. Reduce the heat, and remove the pan as soon as the liquid begins to thicken.

4 Wet a jelly mould and pour in the jelly. Chill for at least 2 hours, or until set. Turn out onto a serving plate, and decorate with fresh flowers, if you like.

--- COOK'S TIP ---

Vegetable gelatine powder contains carrageen, a sea vegetable that has similar setting properties to the animal-derived gelatine. Agar-agar is another seaweed that can be used in place of carrageen, and is available in strips or flakes. Substitute 15ml/1 tsp agar-agar flakes for the vegetable gelling powder in this recipe, if you prefer.

--- NUTRITION NOTES ---

Per portion (if serving 4):

Energy	135kcals/576kJ
Protein	5.1g
Fat	0.0g
Saturated Fat	0.0g
Carbohydrate	30.5g
Fibre	0.2g
Iron	0.6mg
Calcium	37mg

Mixed Berry Tart

The orange-flavoured pastry is delicious with the creamy filling and fresh summer berries. Decorate this tart with finely shredded orange rind and serve with vanilla soya ice cream.

INGREDIENTS

Serves 8

For the pastry
225g/8oz/2 cups unbleached plain flour
115g/4oz/½ cup vegan margarine
finely grated rind of 1 orange, plus extra to decorate

For the filling
300ml/½ pint/1¼ cups thick soya yogurt
finely grated rind of 1 lemon
10ml/2 tsp icing sugar
675g/1½lb mixed summer berries

1 To make the pastry, sift the flour into a bowl. Add the margarine and rub with your fingers until the mixture resembles fine breadcrumbs. Add the orange rind and enough cold water to make a soft dough.

2 Knead the dough on a lightly floured work surface until smooth and elastic, then form into a ball, wrap in clear film and chill for 30 minutes.

3 Roll out the pastry and use to line a 23cm/9in loose-based fluted flan tin. Chill for 30 minutes. Preheat the oven to 200°C/400°F/Gas 6 and place a baking sheet in the oven to heat up.

4 Line the pastry with greaseproof paper and baking beans, place on the heated baking sheet and bake blind for 15 minutes. Remove the paper and beans, and bake for 10 minutes more until golden. Leave to cool completely.

5 To make the filling, whisk together the soya yogurt, lemon rind and sugar, then spoon the mixture evenly into the pastry case. Top with the mixed summer berries and sprinkle with the reserved orange rind. Serve the tart with spoonfuls of vanilla soya ice cream.

NUTRITION NOTES	
Per portion:	
Energy	255kcals/1068kJ
Protein	5.5g
Fat	13.8g
Saturated Fat	4.06g
Carbohydrate	29.1g
Fibre	2.7g
Iron	1.2mg
Calcium	64mg

Blackberry Charlotte

A classic pudding, perfect for chilly autumn days. Serve with thick soya cream or a home-made vegan custard.

INGREDIENTS

Serves 4

65g/2½oz/5 tbsp vegan margarine
175g/6oz/3 cups fresh white
  breadcrumbs
50g/2oz/4 tbsp soft brown sugar
60ml/4 tbsp golden syrup
finely grated rind and juice of
  2 lemons
50g/2oz walnut halves
450g/1 lb blackberries
450g/1 lb cooking apples, peeled,
  cored and finely sliced

1 Preheat the oven to 180°C/350°F/ Gas 4. Grease a 450ml/¾ pint/scant 2 cup dish with 15g/½oz/1 tbsp of the margarine. Melt the remaining margarine and add the breadcrumbs. Sauté for about 5–7 minutes, until the crumbs are crisp and golden. Leave to cool slightly.

2 Place the sugar, syrup, lemon rind and juice in a small saucepan and gently warm them. Add the crumbs.

3 Process the walnut halves until they are finely ground.

4 Arrange a thin layer of blackberries in the bottom of the dish. Top with a thin layer of crumbs.

5 Add a thin layer of apple, topping it with another thin layer of crumbs. Repeat the process with another layer of blackberries, followed by a layer of crumbs. Continue until you have used up all the ingredients, finishing with a layer of crumbs. The mixture should be piled well above the top of the dish because it shrinks during cooking. Bake for 30 minutes, until the crumbs are golden and the fruit is soft. Serve warm.

NUTRITION NOTES	
Per portion:	
Energy	484kcals/2028kJ
Protein	7.0g
Fat	23.0g
Saturated Fat	5.6g
Carbohydrate	66.5g
Fibre	6.4g
Iron	2.3mg
Calcium	126mg

Rhubarb and Orange Crumble

This tangy fruit crumble is extra delicious with home-made dairy-free custard. The almonds give the crumble topping a nutty taste and crunchy texture.

INGREDIENTS

Serves 6
900g/2 lb rhubarb, cut in 5cm/2in lengths
75g/3oz/6 tbsp caster sugar
finely grated rind and juice of 2 oranges
115g/4oz/1 cup plain flour
115g/4oz/½ cup vegan margarine, chilled and cubed
75g/3oz/6 tbsp demerara sugar
115g/4oz/1¼ cups ground almonds

1 Preheat the oven to180°C/350°F/ Gas 4. Place the rhubarb in a shallow ovenproof dish.

2 Sprinkle the caster sugar over the rhubarb and add the grated orange rind and orange juice.

3 Sift the flour into a mixing bowl and add the margarine. Rub the margarine into the flour until the mixture resembles breadcrumbs.

4 Add the demerara sugar and ground almonds and mix well.

NUTRITION NOTES	
Per portion:	
Energy	441kcals/1838kJ
Protein	7.4g
Fat	26.8g
Saturated Fat	6.20g
Carbohydrate	45.4g
Fibre	4.1g
Iron	1.7mg
Calcium	223mg

5 Spoon the crumble mixture over the fruit. Bake for 40 minutes, until the top is browned and the fruit is cooked. Serve warm.

BREADS AND BAKING

Home-made breads are simply unbeatable. The taste of the bread and

the wonderful aroma that fills your kitchen as it bakes will amply

justify the time spent making it. What is more, using wholemeal and

unbleached flour will ensure your bread is nutritious, unlike the many

vitamin-depleted bread products available commercially. Vegan bakes

and biscuits – including savoury scones, cookies, muffins and cakes –

make the most of soya products and wholefood flavourings.

Focaccia

This is a flattish bread, originating from Genoa in Italy, made with flour, olive oil and salt. There are many regional variations, including stuffed varieties, and versions topped with onions, olives or herbs.

INGREDIENTS

Makes 1 loaf
25g/1oz fresh yeast
400g/14oz/3½ cups strong plain flour
10ml/2 tsp salt
75ml/5 tbsp olive oil
10ml/2 tsp coarse sea salt

1 Dissolve the yeast in 120ml/ 4fl oz/½ cup warm water. Allow to stand for 10 minutes. Sift the flour into a large bowl, make a well in the centre, and add the yeast, salt and 30ml/2 tbsp oil. Mix in the flour and add more water to make a dough.

2 Turn out on to a floured surface and knead the dough for about 10 minutes, until smooth and elastic. Return to the bowl, cover with a cloth, and leave to rise in a warm place for 2–2½ hours until the dough has doubled in size.

3 Knock back the dough and knead again for a few minutes. Press into an oiled 25cm/10in tart tin, and cover with a damp cloth. Leave to rise for 30 minutes.

4 Preheat the oven to 200°C/ 400°F/Gas 6. Poke the dough all over with your fingers, to make little dimples in the surface. Pour the remaining oil over the dough, using a pastry brush to take it to the edges. Sprinkle with the salt.

5 Bake for 20–25 minutes, until the bread is a pale golden colour. Carefully remove from the tin and leave to cool on a rack. The bread is best eaten on the same day, but it also freezes very well.

NUTRITION NOTES	
Per loaf:	
Energy	1858kcals/7837kJ
Protein	46.0g
Fat	60.5g
Saturated Fat	8.66g
Carbohydrate	301.2g
Fibre	12.4g
Iron	8.6mg
Calcium	560mg

Olive Bread

Olive breads are popular all over the Mediterranean. For this Greek recipe use rich oily olives or those marinated in herbs rather than the canned ones.

INGREDIENTS

Makes 2 loaves
2 red onions, thinly sliced
30ml/2 tbsp olive oil
225g/8oz/1¾ cups pitted black or
　green olives
800g/1¾lb/7 cups strong plain flour
7.5ml/1½ tsp salt
20ml/4 tsp easy-blend dried yeast
45ml/3 tbsp each roughly chopped
　parsley, coriander or mint

1 Fry the onions in the oil until soft. Roughly chop the olives.

2 Put the flour, salt, yeast and parsley, coriander or mint in a large bowl with the olives and fried onions and pour in 475ml/16fl oz/ 2 cups hand-hot water.

3 Mix to a dough using a round-bladed knife, adding a little more water if the mixture feels dry.

4 Turn out on to a lightly floured surface and knead for about 10 minutes. Put in a clean bowl, cover with clear film and leave in a warm place until doubled in size.

5 Preheat the oven to 220°C/ 425°F/Gas 7. Lightly grease two baking sheets. Turn the dough on to a floured surface and cut in half. Shape into two rounds and place on the baking sheets. Cover loosely with lightly oiled clear film and leave until doubled in size.

NUTRITION NOTES	
Per loaf:	
Energy	1515kcals/6413kJ
Protein	44.8g
Fat	21.7g
Saturated Fat	4.3g
Carbohydrate	287g
Fibre	15.7g
Iron	9.2mg
Calcium	608mg

6 Slash the tops of the loaves with a knife then bake for 40 minutes or until the loaves sound hollow when tapped on the bottom. Transfer to a wire rack to cool.

Polenta and Pepper Bread

Full of Mediterranean flavour, this satisfying, sunshine-coloured bread is best eaten while still warm, drizzled with olive oil.

INGREDIENTS

Makes 2 loaves
175g/6oz/1½ cups polenta
5ml/1 tsp salt
350g/12oz/3 cups unbleached strong plain flour, plus extra for dusting
5ml/1 tsp bicarbonate of soda
5ml/1 tsp sugar
7g/¼oz sachet easy-blend dried yeast
1 red pepper, roasted, peeled and diced
15ml/1 tbsp olive oil

1 Mix together the polenta, salt, flour, sugar and yeast in a large bowl. Stir in the diced red pepper until it is evenly distributed, then make a well in the centre of the mixture.

2 Add 300ml/½ pint/1¼ cups warm water and the oil, then mix to a soft dough. Knead the dough on a lightly floured surface for 10 minutes until smooth and elastic. Place in an oiled bowl, cover with oiled clear film and leave to rise in a warm place until the dough has doubled in size.

3 Knock back the dough, knead lightly, then divide in two. Shape each piece into an oblong and place in the tins. Cover with oiled clear film and leave to rise for 45 minutes. Preheat the oven to 220°C/425°F/Gas 7.

4 Bake the bread for 30 minutes until golden – the loaves should sound hollow when they are tapped underneath. Leave on the baking sheet for 5 minutes, then turn out onto a wire rack to cool.

NUTRITION NOTES	
Per loaf:	
Energy	1011kcals/4270kJ
Protein	30.6g
Fat	13.2g
Saturated Fat	1.91g
Carbohydrate	205.2g
Fibre	8.6g
Iron	5.8mg
Calcium	260mg

Wholemeal Sunflower Bread

Sunflower seeds give a nutty crunchiness to this hearty wholemeal loaf. Serve with a chunk of vegan cheese and rich tomato chutney.

INGREDIENTS

Makes 1 loaf
450g/1lb/4 cups strong
  wholemeal flour
2.5ml/½ tsp easy-blend dried yeast
2.5ml/½ tsp salt
50g/2oz/½ cup sunflower seeds,
  plus extra for sprinkling

1 Grease and lightly flour a 450g/ 1lb loaf tin. Mix together the flour, yeast, salt and sunflower seeds in a large bowl. Make a well in the centre and gradually stir in 300ml/½ pint/ 1¼ cups warm water. Mix vigorously with a wooden spoon to form a soft, sticky dough. The dough should be quite wet and sticky, so don't be tempted to add any extra flour.

NUTRITION NOTES

Per loaf:	
Energy	1748kcals/7395kJ
Protein	69.9g
Fat	38.4g
Saturated Fat	4.24g
Carbohydrate	298.8g
Fibre	44.1g
Iron	21.9mg
Calcium	239mg

2 Cover the bowl with a damp dish towel and leave the dough to rise in a warm place for 45–50 minutes or until doubled in size.

3 Preheat the oven to 200°C/400°F/ Gas 6. Turn out the dough on to a lightly floured work surface and knead for 10 minutes until elastic – the dough will still be quite sticky, but resist the temptation to add more flour.

4 Form the dough into a rectangle and place in the loaf tin. Sprinkle the top with sunflower seeds. Cover with a damp dish towel and leave to rise again for a further 15 minutes.

5 Bake for 40–45 minutes until golden. When ready, the loaf should sound hollow when tapped underneath. Leave for 5 minutes, turn out of the tin and cool on a wire rack.

Banana and Cardamom Bread

The combination of banana and cardamom is delicious in this soft-textured moist loaf. It is perfect for tea time, served with vegan margarine and fruit jam.

INGREDIENTS

Makes 1 loaf
150ml/¼ pint/⅔ cup warm water
5ml/1 tsp dried yeast
pinch of sugar
10 cardamom pods
400g/14oz/3½ cups strong white
    flour
5ml/1 tsp salt
30ml/2 tbsp malt extract
2 ripe bananas, mashed
5ml/1 tsp sesame seeds

1 Put the water in a small bowl. Sprinkle the yeast on top, add the sugar and mix well. Leave to stand for 10 minutes.

2 Split the cardamom pods. Remove the seeds and chop them finely.

3 Sift the flour and salt into a mixing bowl and make a well in the centre. Add the yeast mixture with the malt extract, chopped cardamom seeds and bananas.

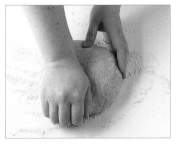

4 Gradually incorporate the flour and mix to form a soft dough, adding a little extra water if necessary. Turn the dough on to a lightly floured surface and knead for 5 minutes until smooth and elastic. Return to the clean bowl, cover with a damp dish towel and leave to rise for 2 hours until the dough has doubled in size.

NUTRITION NOTES	
Per loaf:	
Energy	1536kcals/6540kJ
Protein	48.0g
Fat	6.0g
Saturated Fat	1.2g
Carbohydrate	342.6g
Fibre	13.8g
Iron	7.8mg
Calcium	570mg

5 Preheat the oven to 220°C/425°F/ Gas 7. Grease a baking sheet. Turn the dough on to a lightly floured surface, knead briefly, then shape into a plait. Place the plait on a plastic sheet and cover loosely with a plastic bag, ballooning it to trap the air. Leave until well risen.

6 Brush the plait lightly with water and sprinkle with the sesame seeds. Bake for 10 minutes, then lower the oven temperature to 200°C/ 400°F/Gas 6. Cook for 15 minutes more, or until the loaf sounds hollow when tapped underneath. Cool on a wire rack.

COOK'S TIP

Make sure the bananas are really ripe before using, so that they impart maximum flavour to the bread.

If you prefer, place the dough in one piece in a 450g/1lb loaf tin and bake for an extra 5 minutes.

Chive and Potato Scones

These little scones should be fairly thin with a soft inside and crisp outside. Serve them for breakfast.

Ingredients

Makes 20

450g/1 lb potatoes
115g/4oz/1 cup unbleached
 plain flour, sifted
30ml/2 tbsp olive oil
30ml/2 tbsp snipped chives
oil, for greasing
salt and freshly ground black
 pepper
vegan spread, for topping (optional)

1 Cook the potatoes in a saucepan of boiling, salted water for about 20 minutes, until tender, then drain thoroughly. Return the potatoes to the clean pan and mash them. Preheat a griddle or frying pan.

2 Add the flour, olive oil and snipped chives with a little salt and pepper to the hot mashed potato in the pan. Mix to a soft dough.

─────── Cook's Tip ───────

Cook the scones over a low heat so that the outsides do not burn before the insides are cooked through.

3 Roll out the dough on a well-floured surface to a thickness of 5mm/¼in and stamp out rounds with a 5cm/2in plain pastry cutter. Lightly grease the griddle or frying pan with oil.

4 Cook the scones, in batches, on the hot griddle or frying pan for 10 minutes, turning once, until they are golden on both sides. Keep the heat low. Serve warm, with a little vegan spread, if you like.

─────── Nutrition Notes ───────

Per scone:

Energy	45kcals/191kJ
Protein	0.9g
Fat	1.2g
Saturated Fat	0.1g
Carbohydrate	8.0g
Fibre	0.4g
Iron	0.2mg
Calcium	9.4mg

Orange Shortbread Fingers

INGREDIENTS

Makes 18

115g/4oz/½ cup vegan margarine
50g/2oz/4 tbsp caster sugar, plus extra
  for dusting
finely grated rind of 2 oranges
175g/6oz/1½ cups unbleached plain
  flour

— NUTRITION NOTES —	
Per shortbread:	
Energy	91kcals/429kJ
Protein	0.9g
Fat	5.3g
Saturated Fat	1.6g
Carbohydrate	10.5g
Fibre	0.3g
Iron	0.2mg
Calcium	14.6mg

1 Preheat the oven to 190°C/375°F/
  Gas 5. Beat the margarine and
sugar together until they are soft and
creamy. Beat in the orange rind.

2 Gradually add the flour and gently
  pull the dough together to form
a soft ball. Roll the dough out on
a lightly floured surface until about
1cm/½in thick. Cut it into fingers,
sprinkle over a little extra caster sugar,
prick with a fork and bake for about
20 minutes, or until the shortbread
fingers are a light golden colour.

Double Chocolate Chip Muffins

Everyone loves chocolate and these rich moist muffins have a double dose. They are best when still warm and the chunks of chocolate are melted and gooey.

INGREDIENTS

Makes 8
50g/2oz creamed coconut
300ml/½ pint/1¼ cups boiling water
225g/8oz/2 cups self-raising flour
15ml/1 tbsp baking powder
pinch of salt
40g/1½oz/generous ¼ cup cocoa
 powder
115g/4oz/¼ cup soft light brown
 sugar
60ml/4 tbsp sunflower oil
175g/6oz vegan dark chocolate

NUTRITION NOTES

Per muffin:

Energy	369kcals/1545kJ
Protein	5.0g
Fat	17.3g
Saturated Fat	8.61g
Carbohydrate	51.4g
Fibre	2.9g
Iron	2.1mg
Calcium	147mg

COOK'S TIP

Only cook with good quality dark chocolate that has a minimum content of 50 per cent cocoa solids.

1 Preheat the oven to 180°C/350°F/ Gas 4. Pour boiling water over the creamed coconut, in a bowl. Stir until dissolved, then set aside until cool. Break up the chocolate into chunks.

2 Sift together the flour and baking powder, and add the salt and cocoa powder. Stir in the sugar.

3 Make a well in the centre and pour in the dissolved coconut and oil. Mix well. Stir in the chocolate.

4 Spoon the mixture into 8 paper muffin cases set in a muffin tray and bake for 15 minutes. Transfer the muffins to a wire rack to cool.

Date and Orange Oat Cookies

The fragrant aroma of orange permeates the kitchen when these cookies are baking. Orange is a classic partner with dates and both add a richness to the crumbly oat biscuits.

INGREDIENTS

Makes 25
150g/5oz/¾ cup soft dark brown sugar
150g/5oz/10 tbsp vegan margarine
Finely grated rind of 1 unwaxed
    orange
150g/5oz/1¼ cups self-raising
    wholemeal flour, sifted
5ml/1 tsp baking powder
75g/3oz/¾ cup medium oatmeal
75g/3oz/½ cup dried dates, roughly
    chopped

--- VARIATIONS ---

Replace the dates with dried chopped apricots, raisins or figs.

1 Preheat the oven to 180°C/350°F/ Gas 4. Line 2 baking sheets with greaseproof paper. Place the sugar and margarine in a bowl and beat together until light and fluffy. Mix in the orange rind.

2 Fold in the flour, baking powder and oatmeal. Add the dates and mix until combined.

3 Place heaped tablespoonfuls of the mixture onto the baking sheets, spacing them well apart to allow the mixture to spread. Bake in the oven for 15-20 minutes until golden.

4 Leave to cool slightly, then transfer the cookies to wire racks to cool completely.

--- NUTRITION NOTES ---

Per cookie:

Energy	106kcals/4444kJ
Protein	1.3g
Fat	5.3g
Saturated Fat	1.75g
Carbohydrate	14.3g
Fibre	0.9g
Iron	0.5mg
Calcium	12mg

Pineapple and Ginger Upside Down Cake

A light and moist cake that has a sticky ginger glaze. It is superb as a dessert served with home-made dairy-free custard or thick soya cream.

INGREDIENTS

Serves 8

20g/¾oz/1½ tbsp vegan margarine
2 pieces stem ginger, chopped, plus
    60ml/4 tbsp syrup
432g/1lb can pineapple pieces in
    natural juice, drained
250g/9oz/2¼ cups wholemeal
    self-raising flour
15ml/1 tbsp baking powder
5ml/1 tsp ground ginger
5ml/1 tsp ground cinnamon
115g/4oz/½ cups soft light brown
    sugar
250ml/8fl oz/1 cup soya milk
45ml/3 tbsp sunflower oil
1 banana

NUTRITION NOTES	
Per portion:	
Energy	279kcals/1172kJ
Protein	5.3g
Fat	7.5g
Saturated Fat	1.44g
Carbohydrate	50.7g
Fibre	3.1g
Iron	2.4mg
Calcium	59mg

1 Preheat the oven to 180°C/350°F/ Gas 4. Grease and line a 20cm/ 8in cake tin. Melt the margarine in a small pan and stir in the ginger syrup, heat over a high heat until thickened. Pour the mixture into the prepared cake tin and level the surface.

2 Arrange the stem ginger and one-third of the pineapple pieces in the bottom of the tin.

3 Sift together the flour, baking powder and spices into a bowl. Mix in the sugar.

4 Blend together the milk, oil, the remaining pineapple and banana in a food processor or blender until almost smooth, then add the mixture to the flour. Mix until thoroughly combined. Spoon the mixture over the pineapple and ginger pieces in the tin.

5 Bake for 45 minutes until a skewer inserted into the centre of the cake comes out clean. Leave to cool slightly, then place a serving plate over the tin and turn upside down. Serve hot or cold, with home-made custard or soya cream.

Parsnip Cake with Creamy Orange Icing

INGREDIENTS

Serves 10

250g/9oz/2¼ cups wholemeal
    self-raising flour
15ml/1 tbsp baking powder
5ml/1 tsp ground cinnamon
5ml/1 tsp freshly ground nutmeg
130g/3½oz/7 tbsp vegan margarine
130g/3½oz/scant ½ cup soft light
    brown sugar
250g/9oz parsnips, coarsely grated
1 medium banana, mashed
finely grated rind and juice of
    1 unwaxed orange

For the topping

1 x 227g/8oz tub vegan cream cheese
45ml/3 tbsp icing sugar
juice of 1 small orange
fine strips of orange peel

1 Preheat the oven to 180°C/350°F/
Gas 4. Lightly grease and line the
base of a 900g/2lb loaf tin.

2 Sift the flour, baking powder and
spices into a large bowl. Add any
bran remaining in the sieve.

3 Melt the margarine in a pan, add
the sugar and stir until dissolved.
Make a well in the flour mixture, then
add the melted margarine and sugar.
Mix in the parsnips, banana and orange
rind and juice. Spoon the mixture into
the prepared tin and level the top with
the back of a spoon.

4 Bake for 45-50 minutes until a
skewer inserted into the centre
of the cake comes out clean. Allow
to cool before removing from the tin.

5 For the topping, beat together
the cream cheese, icing sugar,
orange juice and strips of orange peel,
until smooth. Spread the topping
evenly over the cake.

NUTRITION NOTES	
Per portion:	
Energy	257kcals/1074kJ
Protein	4.0g
Fat	11.7g
Saturated Fat	3.72g
Carbohydrate	36.2g
Fibre	3.5g
Iron	1.6mg
Calcium	54mg

INFORMATION FILE

USEFUL ADDRESSES

UNITED KINGDOM
Animal Aid
7 Castle Street
Tonbridge
Kent TN9 1BH
Tel: (01732) 365 446

Animal Liberation Front
BCM Box 1160
London WC1 3XX

**British Union for the Abolition
of Vivisection**
16a Crane Grove
London N7 8LB
Tel: (0171) 700 4888

Compassion in World Farming
5a Charles Street
Petersfield
Hampshire GU32 3EW
Tel: (01730) 264 208

Friends of the Earth
26 Underwood Street
London N1 7JQ
Tel: (0171) 490 1555

National Anti-Vivisection Society
261 Goldhawk Road
London W12 8EU
Tel: (0181) 846 9777

**PETA (People for the Ethical
Treatment of Animals)**
PO Box 3169
London NW1 2JF
Tel: (0171) 388 4922

The Vegan Society
7 Battle Road
St Leonards-on-Sea
East Sussex TN37 7AA
Tel: (01424) 427 393

The Vegetarian Society
Parkdale, Dunham Road
Altrincham
Cheshire WA14 4QG
Tel: (0161) 928 0793

Vegan Business Connection
180 Mansfield Road
Nottingham NG1 3HW
Tel: (0115) 958 5666

Vegfam
The Sanctuary
near Lydford
Devon

**World Society for the Protection
of Animals**
2 Langley Lane
London SW8 1TH
Tel: (0171) 793 0540

CANADA
**Canadian Vegans for Animal
Rights**
c/o General Delivery
Port Berry
Ontario LOB 1NO
Tel: (416) 985 3308

Canada EarthSave Society
Suite 103–1093 West Broadway
Vancouver
BC V6H 1E2
Tel: (604) 731 5885

AUSTRALIA
**Organization for Farm Animal
Liberation**
PO Box E65
East Parramatta
NSW 2150
Tel: (02) 683 5991

Vegan Australasian Network
PO Box 429 Twantin
QLD 4565

Vegan Society of Australia
PO Box 85
Seaford
VIC 3198
Tel: (03) 786 6192

Vegan Society of Brisbane
PO Box 400
South Brisbane
QLD 4101

**Vegan Society of New South
Wales**
12 Eastview
Greenwich
NSW 2007
Tel: (02) 436 1373

Vegan Society of Queensland
36 Hargreaves Road
West End
QLD 4101

SELECTED BIBLIOGRAPHY

Animal Factories, Jim Mason and Peter
Singer (Crown, New York, 1980)

Animal Liberation: A Graphic Guide,
Lori Gruen, Peter Singer and David
Hine (Camden Press, 1987)

Animal Rights and Human Obligations,
Tom Regan and Peter Singer (Prentice
Hall, New Jersey, 1976)

Animals, Politics and Morality, Robert
Garner (MUP, 1993)

The Civilised Alternative, Jon Wynne-
Tyson (Centaur Press, 1986)

Food Fit for Humans, Frank Wilson
(Daniel, 1975)

Food for a Future, Jon Wynne-Tyson
(Centaur Press, 1979)

In Defence of Living Things, Christine
Townend (Wentworth, Sydney, 1980)

The Moral Status of Animals, Stephen
R.L.Clark (OUP, 1977)

The Philosophy of Compassion, Esmé
Wynne-Tyson (Centaur Press, 1970)

Vegan Nutrition, Gill Langley (The
Vegan Society, 1995)

Why Vegan, Kath Clements (GMP,
1995)

INDEX